HORSES, TRUMPETS & SEALS

Lyston
Consultancy & Enterprises LLC

Apostle Steve Lyston

Horses, Trumpets & Seals

Library of Congress Control Number: 2022931516
ISBN: 978-1-7320762-9-7

This book was printed in Columbia, South Carolina in the United States of America

DEDICATION

This book is dedicated to the Father, the Son and the Holy Spirit – The Equipper of His saints.

This book is dedicated to all the End-Time Fivefold workers, the faithful servants in the Body of Christ and every end-time remnant who wants to have a deeper relationship with God.

To every secular leader who truly seeks the wisdom of God to lead well.

THANK YOU

To God The Father, Jesus Christ The Son and to The Holy Spirit of God for His continued faithfulness, guidance, strength, grace and favor upon my life and for His goodness over me and my family.

To my family – Michelle, Shevado, Hannah, and Joshua Lyston.

To Bishop Dr. Doris Hutchinson for her unwavering faith, faithfulness and prayerful support.

To Pastor Sophia DiMuccio, Minister Marsha Hill, Deaconess Sandra Staple for their support.

To Mrs. Marsha McCormack

To Mr. Johann Williams

To Pastor Omanso Jolly

To The RWOMI Watchman Team

TABLE OF CONTENTS

FOREWORD

Never before in history have we seen times like the present, and the Biblical Prophecies are being fulfilled right in our midst – before our very eyes. We seem to be in the last few scenes of the final act leading up to the great battle scene before the protagonist enters stage right to bring the final act to glorious, victorious completion.

Many shy away from reading the Book of Revelation because they are either afraid to read its content or feel overwhelmed when they read it. Some read the Book of Daniel only to find the details of a special fast, or to be reminded of the story of Daniel in the Lion's Den, or about Shadrach, Meshach and Abed-Nego in the fiery furnace. Yet what many don't realize is that by not reading the Books of Revelation, Daniel and other such Books of the Bible others shy away from, they are robbing themselves of the opportunity to identify and extract key end time strategies that can be critically beneficial to all and particularly to members of the Body of Christ.

Could it be that the enemy of our souls wants to steer us away from receiving the Divine Revelations contained in these books by leveraging fear?

Horses, Trumpets and Seals brings Biblical insight to and shares Divine Revelation with the reader with particular emphasis on the solutions-oriented perspective visible in every chapter.

Enjoy being equipped!

Pastor Dr. Michelle Lyston
Senior Pastor
Restoration World Outreach Ministries Inc (RWOMI)

INTRODUCTION

God created everything perfect. He has given man authority to be good stewards in managing His Creation, man's pride arrogance and rebellion against God has opened the door chaos, catastrophe, debauchery, degradation, increased and intensified climatic activities while nations attempt to exclude God from society. There are always consequences for attempting to legislate God out of the society – which include the sword judgement, pestilence, and famine.

Many try to find solutions while they ignore the Source of solutions – the Creator and Architect – and the Word of God.

Regardless of how low man goes spiritually, and the negative things that have been happening as a result of man's action, 2 Chronicles 7: 13 – 14 still holds true, *"When I shut up heaven and there is no rain, or command the locusts to devour the land, or send pestilence among My people, if My people who are called by My name will humble themselves, and pray and seek My face, and turn from their wicked ways, then I will hear from heaven, and will forgive their sin and heal their land."*

Understanding the meanings behind the Horses, Trumpets and Seals and the end-time happenings will help us to unlock the mysteries of Biblical Economics which can effectively help to guide global economies and allow for good decision-making nationally and individually.

Chapter 1

HORSES, SEALS AND TRUMPETS

Since the beginning of 2020 we have seen many interesting happenings which are all Apocalyptic in nature. We have been warning for years about preparation in dealing with some of what we are now facing. Some happenings are the result of the treatment of the poor within the society; some are due to our constant rebellion against the things of God and His ways; meanwhile others are the fulfillment of Scripture. Look at what has happened.

The Coronavirus Outbreak

While the outbreak began in Wuhan, China, *"The rise in new coronavirus cases outside China, now constitutes a global health emergency, the World Health Organization's Emergency Committee declared on Thursday, calling on all countries to take urgent measures to contain the respiratory disease."* (UN News)

This has the potential to impact the West significantly and particularly within poorer countries who don't have the infrastructure to deal with this outbreak. There are also other outbreaks which have been discovered. The Lassa Fever Outbreak has killed 41 in less than a week in Nigeria. The Nigeria Centre for Disease Control (NCDC) said that from January 1 to January 26 a total of 258 confirmed cases, including five health workers, were reported across 19 states.

Earthquakes And Melting Glaciers

In Antarctica, a block of ice the size of Florida is melting more rapidly. If it melts altogether, or melting speeds up, then global sea levels would rise and potential inundate populated countries. Furthermore, land slippage would take place and famine would be imminent. All that would affect Agriculture, Tourism and Business in general and put further strain on the bankrupt health industry which is the case in many countries.

Unless nations begin to put serious plans in place – stockpile masks and vaccines, millions will die.

For years we have been warning through the Prophetic Word the Lord gives us regarding viruses, vaccines, respiratory illnesses, a skin disease and an eye disease never before seen. We have been telling how nations should prepare to prevent mass deaths, but the words have fallen on deaf ears as many nations are focusing on economic reform, gender issues and policies that come against the poor.

We have seen a significant increase in the number of earthquakes worldwide, particularly in areas which were relatively quiet in that regard. These earthquakes have done infrastructural damage. There are other things that are happening under the sea as a result of these earthquakes – we don't know the full extent of these occurrences.

Earthquakes carry a spiritual significance which include:

- ✓ The Power of God being released upon nations

- ✓ The Judgement of God

- ✓ The Shaking of Foundations and Paradigm Shifts within Government and Administrations

- ✓ Creation of Opportunities and Access

- ✓ Wealth Transfer and Opportunities for the fair distribution of wealth.

God is getting the attention of Global Leaders as many no longer honor Him as God.

Seals And Horses

Revelation 6 – 10 speak to us about certain Apocalyptic happenings that would take place. It speaks of the four (4) horses which symbolize the following.

- ✓ The White horse symbolizes international power and politics, in the form of military conquest and global deception.

- ✓ The Red Horse symbolizes of civil war and strife.

✓ The Black Horse symbolizes of economic disruption, inflation, and shortage - things becoming scarce.

✓ The Pale Horse symbolizes disease, death, and devastation that will break out.

Trumpets

In addition to everything above, we will see the fulfillment of the seven trumpets ranging from vegetation and trees being struck and destroyed, and that will affect, agriculture, aquaculture and horticulture. We will also experience:

1. Major oceanic problems – death of many fishes. Contamination will increase significantly and marine life will be affected which ultimately affects our food – particularly seafood.

2. Fresh water will be affected as they will be polluted by meteorites and as such marine life be disrupted yet again.

3. There will be diseases as a result of the cosmic convulsions similar to Exodus 10: 21

4. There will be global deception particularly in the areas of politics and religion. Non-believers who refuse to repent will be seriously impacted.

5. God will also deal with organizations that promote immorality and those involved in witchcraft, according to Revelation 9: 13 – 21. Many will die.

Then we will see a conclusion of the seven (7) trumpets – the seven (7) fulfillments. Those who reject Grace will pay the price and all attention will be on the nation of Israel.

Regardless of what takes place in our world, there is always hope and the Grace of God. Nations who call upon him and follow His instructions will be favored and spared.

The 3-Day Blackout/Darkness

Many were and still are inquiring about the 3-day blackout being foretold by many from 2020 to date, and the concern is intensifying. It is critical for us to understand the prophetic signs and symbols in these end times.
God is speaking prophetically, but we must recognize that when He speaks it is incumbent upon us to look at His prophetic utterances from various angles in order to get a full understanding of what He is saying.

The 9th Plague

First, we must consult the Word of God to understand the mysteries. For example, in the Book of Exodus, there is already a record of a 3-day darkness that already took place – that was the ninth (9th) plague.

"So Moses stretched out his hand toward heaven, and there was thick darkness in all the land of Egypt three days. They did not see one another; nor did anyone rise from his place for three days. But all the children of Israel had light in their dwellings. Then Pharaoh called to Moses and said, "Go, serve the Lord; only let your flocks and your herds be kept back. Let your little ones also go with you." But Moses said, "You must also give us sacrifices and burnt offerings, that we may sacrifice to the Lord our God. Our livestock also shall go with us; not a hoof shall be left behind. For we must take some of them to serve the Lord our God, and even we do not know with what we must serve the Lord until we arrive there." But the Lord hardened Pharaoh's heart, and he would not let them go. Then Pharaoh said to him, "Get away from me! Take heed to yourself and see my face no more! For in the day you see my face you shall die!" So Moses said, "You have spoken well. I will never see your face again." (Exodus 10: 22 – 29)

The 9th plague of darkness carries a two-fold meaning. First, God was demonstrating His power over the sun-god which was the most potent, religious symbol of Egypt. Second, It was a direct frontal attack on Pharoah himself since he was considered to be the incarnation of the sun god, Amun-Ra. So while Egypt plunged into darkness, all the children of Israel had light in their dwelling. God also did it because Pharoah refused to allow the children of Israel to worship God. Furthermore, He wanted them to go without the resources that would be used to give sacrifice to and celebrate the Lord. God also exposed the fact that Pharoah was no god and the He alone is

16

Jehovah. Furthermore, and Pharoah needed to know that the people of God were required to bring their sacrifice before the Lord.

In Goshen there was light, which symbolizes the Holy Spirit; but there was no light in Egypt. It is possible and scriptural that God can do the same things today. Christians should not be afraid, because we are already light and salt. So, while the world may see darkness because of all the things that they have been doing to oppress and hinder Christians – and as a result of the fact that they have used the COVID-19 pandemic as a means of shutting down the Church and stopping Christians from worshipping and serving God, it is within God's capacity to show "Egypt" His power again with another 3-day blackout.

When we speak of "darkness" we need to look at the definition of darkness. For example, wickedness, evil, gloom, corruption, sin, iniquity, immorality, distress, lack of spiritual or intellectual enlightenment, fear and ignorance are all examples of darkness and in fact define darkness. In addition to this, the words hidden, unknown course of action, lack of direction are also a part of "darkness".

Further to all this, John 11: 10, John 12: 35, Luke 22: 53, 1 Thessalonians 5: 7 are scriptures which exemplify darkness. Also, Genesis 1: 2 helps uys to see that darkness includes being without form and void – so there was lack of order, lack of beauty, chaos, total disorder and by extension, darkness brings division. All of this is possible if the Holy Spirit decides to restrain Himself, and then is where you would have hell on earth. The Holy Spirit is the only One Who gives Life, Light and order. He is the Only One Who can restrain any evil spirit. What would happen then, if the Holy Spirit decides to step back and allow evil to reign? He may want to show us all what it is to be ruled by Satan.

A lack of God's word will bring darkness also. The Holy Spirit reacts to God's Word. The world is passing laws to muzzle true worship and God's worshippers, to shut up the mouths of God's people, because God's word brings light, which is the presence of illumination. Once there is a restriction on the Church – the collective carrier of God's Word, Light and Truth – then we will also see the manifestation of that in the luminary bodies created by God on the fourth (4th) day according to Genesis 1: 14. Also, we will see the manifestation of more viruses, plagues, pestilence and death as these are also part of darkness. All these issues can only be dealt with by the children of light. God is clear in His Word that when there is famine, earthquake, pestilence, or what they call climate change, then 2 Chronicles 7: 13 – 14 is the only solution.

Genesis 1 shows us that God uttered over 10 times - the chapter says "And God Said..." over 10 times, and that is what brought life and order back. The Holy Spirit is the One Who brings life and order in times of death and chaos.

A 3-day blackout can also symbolize the rapture of the church, so when God calls away those who are the light, it means the world would plunge into spiritual darkness.

18

The very thing the world is fighting is the very thing that it needs to escape the darkness.

Communication Blackout

This is also another kind of darkness that can come up on the globe. A Communication Blackout includes the results of an EMP (Electromagnetic Pulse), as well as a cyber-attack, falling meteors or a meteoroid shower - which can have serious effects on satellites, volcanic eruptions – where the ashes would block the sun, geomagnetic storms, space weather, terrorism, war, nuclear strike, large scale accidental system failure, extreme weather, power outage, internet and GPS failures, electrical power outage and phone blackouts, radio blackouts, ionization blackouts, and the effects of space craft re-entering the earth's atmosphere.

Financial Blackout

A financial blackout is real. For example, a scenario where all the banks go down and people lose all their resources and all access to recovery of any kind. That would cause a global riot. It means that all 13 stock markets would go down, supermarkets would run out of food and close down, gas station resources would quickly deplete, governments and government systems would crash, and lawlessness would take over.

It is critical for us to understand symbols. For example:

✓ The Sun symbolizes heat, God, Light, goodness, affliction, persecution, trial (Malachi 4: 2; Mark 4: 6 & 17). F

✓ The Moon symbolizes the Church (true or apostate), to rule, to manifest. So where it is said that the moon will turn to blood, it indicates persecution of the Church. (Mark 13: 24; Acts 2: 20; Genesis 1: 16; 2 Kings 23: 5; Deuteronomy 33: 14 and Isaiah 30: 26)

✓ Day/Light symbolizes knowledge, truth, holiness, righteousness, direction, manifestation, revelation and illumination. [and as we know day is the opposite of night]

God can also flood the world with light so much so that the light is a blackout for the darkness and reveal all the lies and deception which can plunge the earth into darkness.

Read Ephesians 5: 13; John 3: 21; Acts 20: 8; Psalm 119: 103; 1 Corinthians 3: 13; Genesis 1: 4 – 5.

Psalm 91: 6 speaks of darkness and the fact that within the darkness there is pestilence that walks. So, this indicates demonic spirits being released upon the globe. It also speaks of destruction that wastes at noonday. Satan will destroy great multitudes, yet not touching the children of God because we dwell in the secret place wherein there is Light. We also see, in Luke 23: 44 – 45, that there was a blackout over the earth between 12 noon and 3 pm. The entire globe was darkened. This was the time when Jesus bore the penalty of man's sin.

The Sun was darkened – blotted – out for 3 hours. (Psalm 22: 1 – 21; John 10: 17 – 18; Hebrews 9: 14)

If Christians have no light, it means they have run out)of oil. (Remember the 5 wise virgins and the 5 foolish virgins.) The Bible also speaks of:

- ✓ The rulers of darkness of this world. (Ephesians 6: 12)
- ✓ The Battle of Armageddon (Ezekiel 38: 9)
- ✓ Satan and his demons will appear on the earth to battle against God. (Joel 2: 2; Isaiah 24: 22; Isaiah 60: 1 – 2; Psalm 67: 1)

God's people Israel There will be darkness in the great tribulation especially when the Church is raptured. The world will have no light. It is critical for the unsaved to surrender to the Lord quickly to enjoy the Light.

Apocalyptic Happenings

Finally, the last darkness is that which surrounds the Apocalyptic happenings.

Based on the Scriptures, only God has the power to block the sun which He has already said He would do in the end-time to bring man into repentance. (Job 9: 7)

Isaiah 13: 10 – 16 tells us that it will be judgement on the Babylonians for the evil that they do on the earth. Read Joel 2 and Amos 8: 9 which says, "And it shall come to pass in that day," says the Lord God, "That I will make the sun go down at noon, And I will darken the earth in broad daylight;"

No one would want to see a global heatwave and a total blackout at midday throughout the world.

Matthew 24: 29 says, "Immediately after the tribulation of those days the sun will be darkened, and the moon will not give its light; the stars will fall from heaven, and the powers of the heavens will be shaken."

Is it that the enemy wants to create a false tribulation before the real one in order to mislead the people of God or deceive people regarding the breaking of the 6th seal which will bring cosmic catastrophe affecting 7 classes of men? If we interfere with the sun, what will happen in places like India and other places affected by heat and water problems?

Mandatory Vaccines And The Four Horsemen

It is interesting that everyone has jumped on the "Mandatory Vaccination" train. But then, we already knew this was coming since the Lord revealed it through several of our prophecies from the Lord. The Lord even told us that the vaccination would not work!

Here are some questions that we need to ask:

- Are "Viruses and Vaccination" the new products on the market?

- Will more viruses be created for more vaccines to come on stream?

- How can we deal with plagues and viruses without Christ's blood?

- Are different variants the results of failed vaccines?

- Are there checks done on our environment and its air quality?

- Is there major policing being done in the area of aeronautics?

- Are there global investigations on the health industry globally?

- If vaccines become mandatory for all workers, what will happen to the business sector? Will it crash?

There are many questions to be answered. The areas that are showing increases in the number of COVID-19 cases only reveals that scientists have failed.

Experts have tried masks, social distancing, quarantines, lockdowns, testing and tracking, vaccination and it is now getting worse. They have reopened and are now locking everything down again.
Now, if all that they are doing is not working, it simply means that testing is still going on. Even if all 8 billion people were to be vaccinated, what guarantee is there

that change will occur? Should something else breakout, will there be an offering more vaccines?

The role of the scientists is to come with facts. However, they have shown that they are not credible, particularly since they have allowed their field to receive its own "jab" of financial greed and political influence.

What Mandatory Vaccinations Will Cause

Mandatory Vaccinations will cause a crash within the marketplace, travel industry, tourism will be wiped out, and also trigger the emergence of the four (4) horsemen and the vial judgement in Revelation 17.

It may also bring about, as prophesied in Revelation, a loss of ¼ of the current, approximately 8 billion people on the planet. That is a total of approximately 2 billion people – 2 billion souls. Is this what they want now?

Recognizing the effort of the political leaders globally, to afford mandatory "jabs" to the global population – if they extended this much effort to bring the peoples of the nations into atonement to bring about a cure (2 Chronicles 7: 13 – 14) and be truthful, wouldn't the world be in a better position than it is currently? If they would put this much effort into having 3 days of atonement for healing to come to the nations, would there have been better results for the globe?
While Revelation 6: 7 – 8 reveals the opening of the fourth seal – the pale horse, which will bring death and disease, and over a fourth of the earth's inhabitants would go.

Revelation 6: 1 – 2 also speaks of the white horse which symbolizes international power, politics and deception, as many prophetic persons may believe that this is what is happening now. However, regardless of what is prophesied, it is the responsibility of nation leaders to lead the people into atonement to avoid the unlocking of the other 2 seals before the time, as they will bring starvation and famine upon the globe.

What Christians Should Do

Christians should use the pandemic as a dress rehearsal for the bigger picture. Christians should not be surprised that many of them will be tested. Some will even lose their jobs. It will be about allegiance and that is what the "666" is all about. The Health industry and "Big Tech" are rising with power and influence – the beast, and we also see revelation 13 being played out right before our eyes in the form of mandatory vaccination – not being able to buy or sell without the mark.

Likewise, we are now seeing the five wise and the five foolish unfolding in our midst. The key thing will be – Who will trust in the end-time – God or man? Who is truly your source? In Whom should we have faith, God or man?

Can God protect you? This is a question many Christians will need to answer.

In Egypt, during the time of Moses, there were plagues of boils, water turned to blood (blood carries diseases) and the Children of Israel, who dwelled in Egypt, had to rely on the instructions given by the Lord through His servants in order to avoid being plagued themselves by the then "pandemic" of the day. Does technological advancement and modernization determine whether we listen to God's instructions and servants or not? Do they determine how much we listen to the instruction of the Lord or listen to Him at all?

Chapter 2

APOCALYPTIC COUNTDOWN

For all those who doubt what the Word of God says about Apocalyptic happenings, by now the happenings of the day are undeniably visible and very telling concerning our closeness to the Apocalypse and all that it entails.

Yahoo! News reported that, "...He (President Trump) moved a small contingent of American troops from the Syrian-Turkish border, signaling to Turkey that it could begin an assault on territory held by Kurdish guerrillas. And within days the assault began, with Turkish air and ground forces attacking towns along the border..." It was also reported that "...over 60,000 people have fled their homes in northern Syria since Wednesday." If nothing else, this is an indicator of the closeness of the fulfillment of Ezekiel 38 – 39. Without a doubt, the goal will be, and alliances will be formed among Russia, Iran and Turkey. Israel will be the target and Iran has said many times that their goal is to eliminate Israel. Incidentally, September 17, 2019 saw all those leaders meeting together; and now we are seeing Turkey advance into Syria.

Ezekiel 38 – 39 reveals the different world events and attacks that will take place within the Middle East. God will judge Gog and its allies, using nature – by way of Climate Change – to devastate the land; it will affect their armies. This will happen, as Israel will stand alone because of the betrayal they will experience. Furthermore, fishes, birds, beasts and man will all be affected; pestilence, bloodshed, rain, great hailstones and a massive earthquake will take place that will affect Israel and the region as well. (Ezekiel 38: 19 – 20)

Sovereignty At Stake

As the countdown continues it will be critical to watch four (4) countries that will dominate the world according to Scripture – Russia, China, Turkey and Iran. The number 4 is very important regarding end-time events. For example, the 4 horsemen in Revelation, the 4 Cardinal Points (North, South, East and West). Many persons are asking, what will happen to America in the end time. I believe that America's influence will be minimal, and that will be determined by who leads the nation and what choices they will make. Money and power will be the order of the day; and something as simple as the statement of the National Basketball Association (NBA) General Manager regarding Hong Kong can turn the tide against the economic growth of the United States. We are now seeing fear among those in business and positions of influence because they are fearful of the possible fallout that could occur as a result. So, they can't speak freely!

I am interested to know how sovereign nations who borrow money from other nations will be affected in the areas of human rights decision-making, economic development, and religious rights – especially in the Caribbean. Will they be able to vote against the issues they disagree with going forward? The UN is now in a financial crisis as they need US$1.4 billion for its Administrative costs alone, because many member states have not been paying. Will they now be forced to lean to a particular direction in exchange for cancellation of debts? How will the UN Charter – the very purpose for which it was formed – be affected?

The Signs of the Times

In addition to all that, there are many happenings that point to the countdown to the major climax of our time. In the USA, Democratic presidential hopeful Beto O'Rourke stated "he would strip the Catholic Church, most evangelical churches, practically every mosque and all related institutions of any tax exemptions and government benefits..." if they refuse to perform same-sex marriages.

In Atlanta, they reported finding fish that can breathe on land.

In Chile they experienced the worst drought in 60 years, with the death of over 160,000 farm animals.

Critical problems arose BREXIT problems are arising (critical to the End Time)

Some nations are running out of water without replenishment

USA continues to experience the highest level of Sexually Transmitted Diseases

Suicide rates are increase rapidly

Increasing numbers of nations are being mined and plundered for their resources

Our health is being assaulted with plastic/fake food increasing in the marketplace, tissue paper being shaped into pills for people to ingest; fish being sold with fake eyes glued to them to make them look fresher, fake vegetables, and water that turns into gel when exposed to natural air.

The countdown has started.

Climate Change: An Apocalyptic Event

With all the great effort being made by various nations to address the issue of climate change, and awareness that the media is attempting to bring to the topic, there are some key elements that are missing in addressing what is taking place.

Despite man's best efforts, we cannot separate the natural, scientific and spiritual connection that exists between man, the entire Universe and God. Luke 21: 25 says, "And there will be signs in the sun, in the moon, and in the stars; and on the earth distress of nations, with perplexity, the sea and the waves roaring;"

We are seeing these six (6) occurrences taking place in the earth like never before. The "Red Tide" in parts of

Florida, earthquakes in diverse places, volcanic eruptions, floods displacing hundreds of thousands of hurricanes occurring close to places that don't usually get such happenings, rare fire tornadoes and other fires raging all over, and the Pacific Ocean being 10 degrees warmer than usual. All these together have the potential to bring about a global famine (food and water will be the new gold.)

Man's Contribution

Negative declarations/words, as well as alternative lifestyles, greed, unrighteousness, crime, violence, abortion, witchcraft, the worship of the universe and its contents instead of the Creator all have their consequential effect on the earth. (Psalm 148). Man has to remember that the very Universe depends on the Creator for its function and sustenance. Injustice, breaking Spiritual laws, and the way we treat the poor are just as important and consequential.

Science

If the Bible tells us that God is shortening the day for the sake of the elect, then it also means that the earth's axis would also be shifted. That would affect every aspect of nature. The creation of the Universe occurred by the Word spoken by God. So any repairing or restoration that would take place must be through the Word. Hebrews 11: 3 reminds us of this – look more deeply at the word "framed" in that Scripture.

Whenever we try to legislate God's Word out of our schools, workplaces and the environment, it will impact negatively on the climate. Man's actions affect the earth, climate, air, ocean, and very soon will cause a greater problem with our local and global communication systems.

God created a perfect climate/cosmos, however, man's actions created negative impact. Similarly, God created the rainbow – a symbol to man that He is the scientific "cure" for the earth and all within.
When we cut down our trees and don't replace them, or run toxic waste into the rivers and oceans, or interfere with the atmosphere, then we will continue to have more problems.

When we erect altars and statues to worship instead of worshipping the Almighty Creator, it will negatively affect us.

The Scientific Approach

Many scientists today are manipulating the weather, many exploring it in space. Creating and setting up systems for dominion and control. As we see in the Book of Genesis the Tower of Babel. Most of these research that are carried out, the source is not true or the spirit of God but other sources. Most of these will create more destruction Globally which includes heatwaves, flooding, problem with lungs, skin problems. Millions will die unless man seek God for wisdom, Knowledge and

Understanding. Scientist knowledge is limited without God.

Oftentimes, scientists are utilizing demonic sources to get knowledge an understanding, some are even resorting to the use of robots and different technology. While Daniel speaks of knowledge increasing in the End Times, knowledge without God, will bring a global explosion - a global crash of system. It will bring Nations into war.

Danger Ahead

There are many that are promoting artificial intelligence, but this will bring great chaos globally. For example, nations that are armed with nuclear weapons are in danger of nuclear unsolicited activation that may take place including hacking. Most of these systems will bring man into greater bondage. When man rejects the creator and begin to worship the creation then we will have a problem. Satan always want to be sovereign that is his greatest plan. There is only one Sovereign God, who is the Most High (Psalm 91). Satan has fooled many to think that they have dominion over man. God has never given man dominion over men, but over the earth. He established government to establish law and order not dominion over man.

Laws And Systems

Globally, governments must be careful that the laws and systems that they are establishing is not to have dominion over man. Jesus is the only man that has that authority for man to worship him. As a result, worship only belongs to Jesus. Many governments globally are instating biometrics and data collection systems and software to control man and their movements. Just as it was in the day of Nimrod (Genesis 11), where man, trying to access the things of heaven and rule over man without coming through God. The result brings what we call language break up or confusion of the language of man – global confusion. We are seeing that many are now journeying into space to establish different space weapon and other communication systems which will come to naught. As God has done it in Genesis 11, we will see God do it again.

Divination

We must recognize that the accessing of the things of the heavens and the heavenly bodies can only come through the Holy Spirt. The Holy Spirit is the only one that qualifies to reveal the things of God to man. No other source is God. Obtaining information illegally can get us wrong information; divination is one such example. Accessing information through divination will bring curses, death, crash of systems. We must stop building an illusion on illegal information and begin to build on the rock, not on sand.

God's Originality

Satan has never designed anything original; everything is God's original designed by God who has the original print. All the enemy does is copy the wrong things and using it to create chaos in the world. He is creating the problem and then comes up with artificial solutions to have man in bondage. Glory, honor, and power comes from the creator. Any system that excludes God will be a failure. It is critical for us to stick to the original design. We have seen the enemy trying to tear down everything in society while creating fake things. Example, fake foods, fake body parts, fake gender even trying to change the DNA of persons as well as animals. Everything is getting fake. Even the sun man is trying to replace! Many trying to block out the sun, which will bring further death and destruction. No life, no food.

God declared Genesis 1:27 – 28, but Satan is trying to change this scripture. He wants to take away man's right of choice. If God Himself gave man choice, why would the devil refuse to give man choice? Any spirit that does this is the Spirit of the Antichrist. Man should never forget that they were created in the image of God. This means that we must be in the image of God that includes Holiness and Righteousness. God created us to take dominion over the universe which includes the resources within the earth. Which only a few have access to it. Man's power to reign in life will extend only as far as his faithfulness to obey God's laws. (1 Chronicles 29:10-16).

God First and Only

Worship belongs only to God- the True and Living God. We are the only earthly creation He gave each a body, soul and spirit. We as moral beings, whose intelligence, perception, self-determination far exceed any other earthly beings, can hear, see and speak and for this reason, God will hold man accountable for the gifts with which we have been entrusted to do His will.

We must return our focus to the Creator and remember that man was created to worship God only.

Repentance And Unity

There are many nations that have joined forces to create systems so they in order to be gods, as we see in Genesis 11: 5 – 9. What man intended, by uniting in effort, will become a symbol of divine judgement. Man cannot build without God. Many billionaires are coming together to build without God, but they only build to fail. It is critical for man to repent now than ever. Those who want to be independent of God rule will suffer great loss within the end times.

Apocalyptic Events

To truly understand what is happening we must first begin to understand the Book of Revelation. The Seven Seals and the Seven Trumpets which will unfold. (Revelation 7, 8 and 9). These Scriptures speak of the different horses – black, pale, white and gray which speak of economic disruption and inflation which will trigger global famine. They also symbolize disaster, death, oceanic contamination, skin disease, water and food related sicknesses, starvation, devastation, military conflict, communication problems, cosmic catastrophes – which would affect the seven structures of creation and the seven classes of men and cause agricultural, horticultural, and aqua-cultural problems. Then we would see freak storms and winds. So all vegetation will be affected as well. We are seeing more frequent occurrence of falling meteoroids which will destroy much of the marine life and marine commerce.

There is going to be pollution of fresh water (Revelation 8: 10 - 11)

For years I have been calling for strategic plans for storage of water and food and even Jamaica, should not have designated the Caymanas area for building but for water storage and protection of the natural waters there. Water and food will be critical, and we cannot continue to look at climate change from a singular perspective.

Chapter 3

APOSTASY AND SIGNS OF TIMES

2 Timothy 3: 1 – 9 says,

"But know this, that in the last days perilous times will come: For men will be lovers of themselves, lovers of money, boasters, proud, blasphemers, disobedient to parents, unthankful, unholy, unloving, unforgiving, slanderers, without self-control, brutal, despisers of good, traitors, headstrong, haughty, lovers of pleasure rather than lovers of God, having a form of godliness but denying its power. And from such people turn away! For of this sort are those who creep into households and make captives of gullible women loaded down with sins, led away by various lusts, always learning and never able to come to the knowledge of the truth. Now as Jannes and Jambres resisted Moses, so do these also resist the truth: men of corrupt minds, disapproved concerning the faith; but they will progress no further, for their folly will be manifest to all, as theirs also was."

It is critical for everyone, whether believers or non-believers to take note of this particular scripture. We need to focus on the different areas listed by Apostle Paul.

We are indeed in perilous times. Perilous means harsh, savage, difficult, dangerous, fierce, and grievous. As Children of God, we need to begin using the Word of God as a measuring point. When a leader or any Christian embraces an opinion contrary to the Word of

God, they have already fallen into apostasy and should be avoided. (2 Peter 2: 20 – 22), When a leader or any member of the Christian family begins to advocate for sin to become legal, you as a Christian need to avoid that person. Any Christian opinion or leader that is not in line with the Bible should be avoided. Everything a Christian says or does has to be in line with the Word. Once it is not in line, then that person has fallen from Grace. They are already in apostasy, and they need to go back to Calvary. It is very critical who we follow in this end time because we are surely in the end time.

When a Christian leader who is a musician or singer starts to encourage people in New Age Movements, Transcendental Meditation, Yoga, Tattoos, Sexual Immorality, it is time for you to leave that church.

Prophets and their Messages

Galatians 1:8 says, "But even if we, or an angel from heaven, preach any other gospel to you than what we have preached to you, let him be accursed."

Any prophet's message that is promoting any ministerial office more than the office of Jesus Christ, don't follow them! If a prophet is preaching more about how accurate he is, rather than Jesus crucified, risen and ascended – which should be center of the message – don't follow them! No prophets should be exalting themselves above Jesus and the Holy Spirit. Even on flyers we see prophets having 3 or 4 pictures of themselves telling people to come and see them, but nothing is mentioned about Jesus or the Holy Spirit. Furthermore, true prophets draw the attention of the people to Jesus Christ not to themselves. Every prophet must submit to the governing authorities within the local church. They have to be pastored, shepherded and taught. They are not under the old covenant anymore where they are accountable directly to God. There was no church in the Old Testament. Jesus restructured the Church according to Ephesians 4: 11 and 1 Corinthians 12: 27 – 28 which says, "Now you are the body of Christ, and members individually. And God has appointed these in the church: first apostles, second prophets, third teachers, after that, miracles, then gifts of healings, helps, administrations, varieties of tongues."

So, they are set within the local church to establish and build the church. There are many within the Body of Christ teaching false doctrines. Some are even giving themselves names like "Forensic Prophets", "CSI", while others are teaching that accuracy makes one a true prophet – which is not true. Jesus said in Matthew 7: 15-20 which says, "Beware of false prophets, who come to you in sheep's clothing, but inwardly they are ravenous wolves. You will know them by their fruits. Do men gather grapes from thornbushes or figs from thistles? Even so, every good tree bears good fruit, but a bad tree bears bad fruit. A good tree cannot bear bad fruit, nor can a bad tree bear good fruit. Every tree that does not bear good fruit is cut down and thrown into the fire. Therefore by their fruits you will know them.

Always look for the Fruit of the Spirit as in Galatians 5. Watch out to see whether or not they try to break up churches or pull people away. Always ask them, "Who is your Apostle?" If they say they submit to no one but God – RED FLAG!

Watch out for those who say they will release curses and/or send curses back to sender.

God is realigning His Church and putting things back in order, and only those who will line up, will be a part of the end time move. This realignment is also part of the structure being reinforced that the Church be fortified for the end time and move as an army.

Apostasy, Error, And Deception

The manifestation of the Word of God is very visible in these end times. We are seeing Biblical prophecies being fulfilled before our eyes rapidly, while the rest of the globe is focused on the pandemic. There are ever-changing laws, and increased pronouncements and endorsements of every kind taking place. We are seeing apostasy and the Apostate Church being revealed and a general falling away from the truth.

It is critical for the saints to discern like never before. Deception and error are everywhere. The anti-Christ agenda is materializing.

Let it be clear to us all that if a person does not have a strong foundation in the Word of God, they will be deceived. It must also be noted that regardless of the name of your Church, how recognized your

Pastor/Leader may be, if their actions, endorsements, pronouncements are not in line with God's Word, they are false – false prophets, false teachers, false shepherds. The same is also true if they are politicians and/or businessmen. Furthermore, their souls are in danger of hellfire. God will not change His word to suit anyone, any organization nor any nation.

The Apostate Church And The World

The Bible speaks of apostasy, deception and error in the end times. It speaks of the World and the Church – religious and political – coming together to form and unholy alliance. We will see religious, doctrinal, ethical, intellectual, political, sexual, and financial deceptions increasing in these times.

2 Thessalonians 2: 3 tells us, "Let no one deceive you by any means; for that Day will not come unless the falling away comes first, and the man of sin is revealed, the son of perdition,"

Many churches have fallen away and many are on that path if there is no turning. The Bible reminds us in Deuteronomy 27: 17 that it is dangerous to remove the ancient landmarks. God's word is clear on the Family, Gender, Sex, Sin, Holiness, Uncleanness, Israel, Hell and Heaven. Every saint should keep their eyes on the Books of Revelation, and Daniel. (Deuteronomy 4: 2, Deuteronomy 12: 32, Proverbs 30: 5 – 6, 2 Timothy 3: 16, Matthew 24: 35, Galatians 1: 6 – 9, Hebrews 4: 12, Revelation 22: 18 – 19)

It is also critical for the people of God to rely on the Holy Spirit in the end time to help us to identify these deceptions. (John 16: 13). The Holy Spirit is God, and the only One qualified to bring all truth to us; and expose the end time deceptions.

The Bible also reminds us that we will see many deceptions in the end time. Matthew 24: 22 says, "And unless those days were shortened, no flesh would be saved; but for the elect's sake those days will be shortened."

With all the earthquakes taking place and the various shifts in the cosmos, it almost seems as if 24 hours literally got shorter. We are also seeing the Vial Judgments happening globally, the sealing of the saints taking place as well as the Mark of the Beast being issued out.

The Great Whore

Revelation 17: 5 tells us that in this end time we will see a worldwide apostate church that will reject Christ and dishonor God. We now see it taking place.

There are many who are deemed great in the eyes of the world but not in the sight of God. They look good on the outside but they are harlots. A harlot is "an individual who is unfaithful to their wedding vows, but professes to be loyal to Christ, when in fact they cleave to idols, false religions, sin and the ways of the world. We should also take note of the seven churches in the Book of Revelation and beware of the seven horns and ten heads, as well as the revival of the Roman Empire.

Everyone needs to understand and accept the fact that salvation comes only through Jesus Christ – He is the ONLY Way. There is no other way! He is also the only One Who can give us Peace.

The Truth About Apostasy

Based on recent reports in traditional and non-traditional media sources, there are many popular artists and church leaders renouncing the Christian faith including – Author and Former Pastor Joshua Harris and Hillsong leader Marty Sampson. However, this should not be a surprise since the Bible tells us that in the End-Time there would be a great falling away. There are several scriptures in the Bible that speak to us of Apostasy.

There are many who say they are Christians, but they know they are not. Some are simply camouflaging themselves in Christianity, pretending to be a part of the faith, but are like sleepers waiting for the appointed time to rise up, declare their "departure" from the faith, and pull as many souls as they can with them onto the path of eternal death – preparing them for hell.

If Judas had a foundation, there is no way he would have betrayed Jesus. Judas' heart did not let go of the things of the world; and the Word of God says to be a friend to the world is to be an enemy to God.

Signs of Apostasy

As we draw closer to the end of time, we will see many people fall away from the truth of God. We will see false signs, religious deceptions, social and political upheavals, natural calamities, disloyalty and persecution; and sadly, some churches will take a stand to endorse the unclean and sinful things.

We must recognize that Apostasy is not something that happens overnight. There are many who call themselves Christians, but God does not have their heart. Christianity is about your faith in Christ – your total allegiance to Him (through good and bad times). One cannot have allegiance to both Christ and the world at the same time. How can Christians live like the world?

Testing Is Necessary

Every time the Word of God is preached or taught, a lot will receive it with joy, but as soon as persecution and trials come, many fall away. It simply means that those Christians did not have any deep roots in the first place. That is why God tends to carry Christians through testing.

The Lord tests His people with the Word first. Then there are other tests He gives - the Wilderness Test, the Patience Test - to reveal their allegiance and love for Him. That is why the Word says you must deny yourself and take up your Cross daily. You must deny the world and its pleasures. A person who falls into Apostasy, is someone who refuses to carry their Cross daily. Many Christians may comment with their views and how they feel about something, but if it is not in line with the Word of God, then they are carnal.

Costly To Reject The Work of The Spirit

Everyone who calls him/herself a Christian must know that regardless of the level of your popularity or ability to quote many scriptures, that is no indication that God has your heart. Even more so if someone deems him/herself as having knowledge of God, having been a Christian for many years and having "been there and done that". They need to read Hebrews 10: 26 – 31 – one of the most solemn warnings against Apostasy found in the Scriptures.

If someone willfully forsakes Christ, there is no other sacrifice for sin. There are degrees of punishment. If the one who rejects Moses' law suffers the judgement prescribed in Deuteronomy 17: 2 - 6, an apostate from Christianity, will suffer an even worse punishment, for he has treated the Son of God with scorn, regarded His blood as common and unclean, and has insulted the Holy Spirit. So, to insult the Spirit of Grace implies a rejection of the work of the Spirit once it has been experienced.

The book of Revelation tells us what to expect and how things will end. It is not to bring fear, but truth and victory for those who stand in Jesus Christ.

I encourage every Christian who says they are Christians to examine yourselves and begin to get or strengthen your relationship with Christ. You are not of the world you are set apart so you can't be like the world. There are many brands of Christianity out there, but we only have one truth!

Chapter 4

ARE THERE NO DANIELS IN BABYLON?

There are no kingdoms or governments will be able to function effectively without a Daniel. Daniels are needed to serve within the various areas of the political sphere or within any organization, because they will bring balance, clarity, insight and the fear of God which will ultimately bring stability to the governments and nations.

I have seen many leaders – regardless of their good intentions – fall out of favor with both God and the people, because there are no Daniels within the Administration.

The Daniels of today will understand the Times and Seasons and what
to do within that period. Sadly, many are missing it and also missing opportunities. A leader cannot even fight crime and violence and win when they don't even know what they are fighting. As I have said many times, the only solution that seems to be forthcoming is the passing of ineffective laws, and oftentimes laws are not the answers to the issues. In fact, most of these laws make matters worse.

Regardless of the organization, God never leaves a leader without help or assistance. He always makes a way/solution for them to get help. But they have to discern and know when help comes from Him. God is always speaking in dreams and visions to leaders –

whether they believe or not. So it is important for us all to pay attention to the dreams and visions we receive. Thus, one of Daniel's role was to make known the kings demands and determine what God is saying to the king in dreams and visions concerning future events and how they would affect future events. And for the king to fully understand what the Lord is saying, it is imperative for him to begin to test or examine his advisors – recognizing that some of them are soothsayers and cannot interpret the spiritual mysteries.

Recognize that Daniel was superior to all the fellow advisors surrounding the king. They were living luxuriously – yet they were soothsayers, magicians, wise men and astrologers. Despite that, they could not make known the king's demands or interpret the king's dreams. Furthermore, God used that scenario to reveal that spiritual counterfeits are in no category with the wisdom and power of the Holy Spirit.

Many who consider themselves well learned or intellectual or theological superiors may be wondering how this article makes any sense. It may not make sense to them now because of what they see and how they think, but it may make sense when the king calls them up to accountability and they can't deliver.

If God can use four (4) slaves – with their God-given capacity to administrate and grasp technical concepts and language – to serve within an Administration that needed skillful administrative bureaucracy – and allow them to prove to be far superior to their noble counterparts, then the issue is not one of academic qualifications, but one of a willingness to see beyond the natural circumstances and connect on a spiritual level with God for the solutions needed. That is why I always say we should not politicize the problems or think that it takes a political party to solve a problem. Maybe what we need are four (4) Daniel type men, four (4) active ministries, four (4) focused people, four (4) strategies for growth and job creation and/or four (4) products to enhance the nation.

Everyone must know that the destiny and direction of a nation, regardless of man's plans and agendas, God is the only One who controls those matters. So that even where unscrupulous individuals may want to divert the nation according to their desires, God rules in the affairs of men.

Moving Forward

If we as a nation are going to move forward, there are some fundamental things we will need to look past.

We must look past:

- ✓ Politics
- ✓ Color
- ✓ Race
- ✓ Class

And we now have to look at

- ✓ Leadership styles

✓ Layout and Implementation
✓ Waste and Distribution of resources

The poor and the youth must be the priorities within the nation.

We need to stop looking at other nations trying to determine how to adopt their systems – their systems are not for us. We need our own systems and we must seek to see the value within. We need to know what we have – as many nations today don't know that.

So even where we hand over our land to foreign entities and ignore its overall value and importance to the nation, we lose tremendous value on every level.

Recognize that to grow a nation requires the stability of the feet – the masses.
We can't be a "Profit-and-Loss-only" nation – Purpose, Direction and Empowerment of the people are of utmost value and importance, and oftentimes of even greater importance.

Nehemiah: The Type Of Leader Needed For Our Nation And Church

Nehemiah was a leader who feared God. He was a man full of wisdom, one who could not be bought. One who would put his life on the line for his people – who would not tolerate sin and unholiness in the sight of God. A hard worker – diligent, depending totally on God.

Nehemiah 13: 4 – 31 we see where he reforms the house of God, putting people in charge to be accountable and clean up the house of God so that justice would prevail. He was a great leader who feared nothing.

Nehemiah can also be described as a good manager and a good administrator who gets things done. He led by example. He placed people in strategic positions to bring out the best in them that God would be glorified. He had great compassion for the poor. He would work out the solution for their problems then take their problems and a solution to higher authority in a way that they would have no problems granting his requests.

Nehemiah would dedicate any new venture, project, building etc. to God in worship and praise. He would also honor men who served well in the past.
We need to look at the life of Nehemiah as a guide to the reformation of our land.

1) We need to set up a center for our retired clergy, teachers, police, civil servants, so they can continue to impart their wealth of knowledge to the younger generation – possibly in conjunction with the Places of Safety for our nation's youth.

2) We must use our retired church men who served well to:

- ✓ Set up programs/projects for street boys and girls.
- ✓ Set up a school to train them.

- ✓ Set up and run a counseling center (to counsel the abused & prostitutes inner city youth) and focus also on conflict resolution.
- ✓ Select from these retirees, Justices of the Peace.

We need to set apart a day for God. We need to become more rigid on our days of worship and use it to focus on God. **(Nehemiah 10)**. Starting with Christians, they must be more committed on their day of worship.

For almost 20 years I have been saying that Flexi-week works against this kind of focus and will bring a curse upon our nation once implemented, and God will not get the glory and praise He truly deserves. Are we not seeing this today?

The government needs to set up a cess – where on one specific day each year, everyone contributes to a special fund wherein the money will be distributed to the nation's elderly and poor – the furtherance of the work of God in this nation **[example – smaller churches in the rural areas]. (Nehemiah 10: 2).**

Government should carry out a campaign to encourage companies to give to the work of God especially when they make profits. This would be tax deductible.

Nehemiah 8: 1 – 6 states that we must give place to the public reading of scripture as a source of understanding and encouragement.

The crocodile should be removed from our currency - it is a curse. We should encourage our businessmen to carry out fewer transactions on our holy days.

A day must be dedicated each year to the Lord, for the confession of our sins to the Lord, as well as public reading of the Word of God. This day should not fall on a weekend. At this point prayer and fasting would be carried out in the 14 parishes of the nation. **(Nehemiah 9)**

Our government, with the support of the private and public sector, should legislate a Bill that every seven years, all bad debts should be written off. **(See Nehemiah and Deut. 15: 1 - 6)**

All the churches should give the tithes and offerings collected on a specific day to the elderly and poor in the country.

All leaders should be given Nehemiah 5: 14 – 19 to read that they may fully understand the weight of the charge given to them to lead the nation. Then allow God to be the judge.

For peace prosperity and success to be experienced within a nation, it is critical for the gates to be restored, particularly the Dung Gate and the Valley Gate, as outlined in the book of Nehemiah.

Chapter 5

BEWARE OF THE NICOLAITANS

The doctrine of the Nicolaitans is also the doctrine of Balaam – that good works bring salvation. Nicolaitan simply means "having power/victory (control) of the laity". (1 Peter 5: 1 – 3). Recognize, however, that feeding the poor and carrying out charity work is good, but that is not salvation – it is not what gets you to go to heaven.

Salvation means you are saved by grace through faith in Jesus Christ. In other words, you have accepted that Jesus is real, His life on earth and His sacrifice through His death on the Cross are real, His resurrection is real, and you accept Him as Lord of your life. Ephesians 2: 8 – 10 says:

"For by grace you have been saved through faith, and that not of yourselves; it is the gift of God, not of works, lest anyone should boast. For we are His workmanship, created in Christ Jesus for good works, which God prepared beforehand that we should walk in them."

The Nicolaitan doctrine focuses on wealth, title, power, honors and accolades as being the standard for being in right standing with God. It also says you can partake in sin because the law of God is no longer binding. So it abuses and tramples on the Grace of God.

Recognize that while God wants us to have prosperity, it does not indicate that you are with God. In fact, 1 Timothy 6: 10 says,

"For the love of money is a root of all kinds of evil, for which some have strayed from the faith in their greediness and pierced themselves through with many sorrows."

This doctrine has seeped into the Five-fold Ministry and has taken hold. Many Apostles and Prophets today, now want to be as the Episcopalians – wanting to dress and function as they do – thereby compromising their walk, the Gospel and the value of true salvation.

There are false teachers who have taken over the church and Jesus hated false teaching. Read every word for yourself in Revelation 2: 12 – 15.

Nicolaitans work closely with Jezebel, who teaches God's people spiritual adultery or fornication – meaning that while having a relationship with God, they are embracing false doctrines and performing actions opposite to God's Word and instructions.

Revelation 2: 5 – 6 says,

"Remember therefore from where you have fallen; repent and do the first works, or else I will come to you quickly and remove your lampstand from its place— unless you repent. But this you have, that you hate the deeds of the Nicolaitans, which I also hate."

Nicolaitans are also paid prophets who utter curses and seduce God's people into sinning.

Beware of the falsehood of the Nicolaitan doctrine and recognize that true salvation is not by way of works, but by the Way Who is Jesus Christ.

The Government Of God

There are many genuinely righteous people today walking away from the secular industries because they believe that it causes them to compromise their beliefs, and they take with them invaluable contributions to their organizations, groups and the nation. But that is not always the right choice. There is need for light, particularly in the secular world, in order to allow change to come. The absence of light is darkness. There is no such thing as a separation of church and state. There ought not to be a separation of secular and religious. God did not make secular and religious people; he made man, in His own image. It was man who chose separation! The global failure at this point is the lack of light within strategic positions. Those that are light will operate under the government of God.

In order for us to see and experience change, God's government must be seen in all areas – media, politics and finance. It was God's government, in time of recession and famine, which rescued Pharaoh's government. Pharaoh was a secular king, but, Joseph was operating under God's government. In politics, if the administration is operating under God's government, there will be a rebuilding of the wall within the nation. Politicians would walk in integrity and principle and would deal with excessive spending, oppression and engage in self-sacrifice for others to follow, as they lead by example. They would also champion the cause of the poor. They would help those who fell on hard times because of their economic circumstances; as well as those who are victims of human trafficking, prostitution and the sex trade.

The government of God creates an environment for investment and gives the poor an equal opportunity to function in a competitive market, remove exclusivity and criteria that only the rich can meet, and provides a fair tax policy.

Foreign Policy/Tourism

The government of God does nothing – that includes making major decision, developing foreign policies or implementing tourism-based plans – without seeking God's guidance and using His Word as a guideline.

Most of the Caribbean countries, including Jamaica, have made decisions which violate God's Word, and these decisions have set these nations on a course to negative repercussions. Jamaica, for example, has removed all visa restrictions from some countries in order to boost tourism. This will affect the nation's sovereignty in the future, as Jamaica does not have the necessary resources to protect its borders, furthermore, serious moral, security and labor issues still exist, and, they have not addressed the logistics issues overseas, such as setting up more embassies. Opening our borders for the sake of increasing tourism, will create major problems on the nation; problems which we are not equipped to handle. Furthermore, there will be a loss of revenue. The only beneficiaries of such a situation are the various all-inclusive hotels. The poor don't benefit in any way. The country needs to fix the crime problem or screen and collect visa fees at the port of entry.

The government of God is built on the principles of God. We cannot depend on loans and other governments to help us come out of our circumstances; neither can we trust man (Jeremiah 17:5-8). We have to trust God to help us turn things around. We have always heard the Jamaican adage – 'short-cut draw blood'. Well, embargoes do too! Some of the decisions made concerning the nation will bring serious embargoes in the future.

Learn From Nehemiah

In order for lawmakers and politicians to create a new environment, we must rebuild the walls that are broken down. We have to encourage all sectors to unite; rebuilding family values and put laws in place that encourage the building of families.

There needs to be reform to national security and to the justice system.

There needs to be a strengthening of the curriculum to inculcate discipline within our children's studies while they learn the traditional subjects. They need to be taught the implications and repercussions of negative actions – including tattooing, gambling, sex before marriage and the facts about HIV and other sexually transmitted infections. They need to be made to understand that going after gifts from men and women who are not their close family members has the potential to make them victims of human trafficking and the global sex trade.

Don't Be Distracted! Don't Be Deceived!

There are five main types of wind in the Bible – each having a different purpose.

The wind symbolizes the regenerative work of the Spirit of God and it is indicative of His mysterious, penetrating, life-giving and purifying operation.

Always remember:

The **East Wind** carries with it judgement and brings the destruction of the ship, crew, crops and also brings drought, scorching, scattering, wars and riots. It affects the environment negatively through storms, locusts as well as other plagues and disease. It brings confusion and chaos. (Read Ezekiel 27: 26;; Exodus 10: 13, Jonah 4: 8, Exodus 14: 21; Job 27: 21, Isaiah 27: 8, Psalm 78: 26)

The **West Wind** carries with It restoration, redemption, revival, healing and drives away the locusts. (Exodus 10; 19,) It also drives away bad/negative things.

The **North Wind** brings rain (Proverbs 25: 23), awakening and pleasantness. (Songs of Solomon 4: 16).

The **South Wind** brings peace, comfort, stability, protection, heat, energy and food. (Acts 27: 13; Acts 28: 13, Job 37: 17)

Now there is also a type of wind called the **Contrary Wind** (Mark 6) which brings confusion, deception, opposition by the enemy, fear, lies and fights against your purpose and your assignment. That wind comes from the enemy.

Distraction brings deception. Don't be distracted in this season, focus on the Holy Spirit in this season. There are rough times ahead. This is the time for the unsaved and the backsliders to come home.

We do not walk by sight; we walk by faith! Don't look at what you see, because what you see, may not be what you think it is. Backsliders! Sinners! Time's up!
We are in a time where the East Wind, West Wind and the Contrary winds are blowing.

The Heart of The Good Samaritan (Luke 10: 25 – 37)

This is a Scripture that every leader, every Christian, every non-Christian needs to read if we truly want changes in the world, and if we truly want to stomp out anything that is contrary to God's Word. Some of us may say "We know the Law, we practice the Law" but are we doers of the Law. (Law here meaning the Word of God).

The Selfishness That Abounds

Notice that Jesus in response to the lawyer – who was supposed to be an expert in the Law, highlighted the Priest, and the Levite in His parable about the Good Samaritan; and showed that the Priest and the Levite passed the wounded man lying don on the side of the road – stripped and half dead. He was neglected. How many today are doing the same thing, yet we talk about racism, classism and are jumping on the racial injustice system bandwagon courtesy of George Floyd; when you all have different agendas. There are many that you pass daily without taking a second look. Selfishness abounds – that selfishness which is the commanding force of human nature. The Samaritans and the Jews were enemies, but this Samaritan's heart of compassion and mercy (which the world lacks) looked beyond the race, culture, color, and status and saw the person who needed help. We don't have a race problem, we have a heart problem, and our hearts are wicked – the heart that would pass someone who is hurting and in need.

Practice the Law

When George Floyd was alive, struggling, and was in need, why didn't others reach out to help him? Where was all the support then? Where were those who say they know the law and practice the law and have the love of God and the Ten Commandments in their hearts?

Love Your Neighbor

Luke 10: 26 – 29 says, "He said to him, "What is written in the law? What is your reading of it?" So he answered and said, " 'You shall love the Lord your God with all your heart, with all your soul, with all your strength, and with all your mind,' and 'your neighbor as yourself.' " And He said to him, "You have answered rightly; do this and you will live." But he, wanting to justify himself, said to Jesus, "And who is my neighbor?"

We need to remember that our neighbor is not simply those of our own kind – our neighbor runs across racial, cultural, and color lines.

Why didn't the media highlight the years of neglect of the poor and voiceless by those in positions of authority and access to resources?

Change the World

We must stop dividing the people and begin to help the people regardless of skin color.

Instead of continuing to allow Satan to divide us continually on issues of race, sex, and all these issues keeping us from seeing the truth and the real issues, seek the Lord for the Heart of the Good Samaritan and change the world!

We Are In A Revival

With all that is taking place – viruses, locusts and natural disasters – we are also experiencing global recession. This is an indication that we are in the midst of a revival. The works and plans of man's hands without God are coming to an end.

Many times, within the charismatic circles, people say "A revival is coming!" or that they are *doing* a revival. But God is showing this generation what true revival ought to be! Many may think that a revival is the manifestation of certain miracles which cause the preacher/teacher/prophet to become more popular or famous. However, true revival takes place when God becomes the central focus among the saved and the unsaved.

The meaning of the word "revival" is "an instance of something becoming popular, active or important again; an improvement in the condition or strength of something."

Since the COVID-19 pandemic, even the Bible has become a scarce commodity – as many places are out of stock! The desire to go to church, even in the midst of the lockdown – that's revival!   Prior to this, even when you begged someone to go to the House of the Lord with you, they would tell you how busy they were; and work, gym appointments, yoga sessions, and social functions always took precedence over Church. Now, everything that stood in the way of them going to Church services has been shut down and they are ready and willing to go to the House of the Lord to worship.

The Marketplace

The Spirit of Mammon that has taken over the marketplace, trying to legislate the Church out of the globe, and that has been persecuting Christians, subscribes to the New Age Movement and principles. Furthermore, many in our society – doctors, lawyers, educators, and the civil society, are no longer embracing God as they should anymore. Instead they embrace the New Age Movement and the Spirit of Mammon.

Now we see many freely turning to and worshiping the True and Living God without fear. The marketplace will never be the same; and now it will only prosper when they fully employ the Spirit of God and the Principles of God. Prayer will no longer be after the fact and in times of tragedy, but any time – 24 hours per day, 7 days per week, and that is revival! Revelation 18 is in effect and Babylon is fallen – and that is revival. Only those – according to Jeremiah 17: 8 – 9 – who put their trust in God will expand and prosper even in recession – **that is revival**.

The Church

Suddenly, the Church has been transformed – as a result of the virus. God has shown us that the Church is His Bride; and every man-made doctrine or agenda is being uprooted and Jesus Christ will be the center again. God is bringing everyone back to basics. Pastors who did not embrace other pastors based on the size of their church and popularity levels have been reverted to the home for a time of reflection. God is showing us that the center of the church should not be the acquisition of material things, but instead, the focus MUST be on winning souls, helping the poor, evangelism, genuinely expressing love for our fellow man and being the light and salt of the earth as God instructed.

Healing

With the world trying to create vaccines for viruses, the focus will again be on the Healing Ministry that Jesus Christ has given the Church. The plants and the fruits that the pharmaceutical industry has been fighting will now come back to the forefront. Many have already begun to use these natural, unadulterated, unprocessed, God-given items to rebuild their immune systems. Scientists will no longer be gods; but God will be God for His people – and **that is revival!**

The Books of Revelation, Zechariah, Daniel and Psalm 91, in addition to the Blood of Jesus, the Name of Jesus have come to the fore again – and **that is revival!**

Revival

While writing this article today, the Lord said, "It is not if revival is coming – we are in the REVIVAL!" We have prayed for that! We have cried for that – because of the injustice! Now we are seeing the manifestation. We must renew our minds so that we do not pray against what He is doing, but instead pray for His will to be done! We will see His mighty hand this 2020. Watch from now until June 2020 for God's mighty hand. He is leveling the playing field, and He will bring down great opposition, so that His people will cross over. He will bring down every high thing that exalts itself against the knowledge of God. That is why we must continue to pray that the revival continues. This is a God-Revival for His people and only He will get the glory!

Chapter 6

THE EFFECT OF INEFFECTIVE PRAYERS

"So I sought for a man among them who would make a wall, and stand in the gap before Me on behalf of the land, that I should not destroy it; but I found no one." (Ezekiel 22: 30)

With the recent uprising and turmoil now happening worldwide – the wanton murders especially of women and children; and the attacks against churches, and the security threats throughout the globe – many questions must be asked. Such as, with a nation that has the most churches per square mile, why does it seem as if darkness is getting the upper hand?

Let us look at our options. Many of those criticizing the church are attempting to 'legislate' God out of the schools, businesses and the affairs of the nation, while they ask the question 'Where is God?'

One cannot pray effectively in order to bring quick results if there is unforgiveness or wrong motives. We can't be effective in prayer if one is politically-biased; praying blessings for their party while they declare curses on the opposing party. Are we praying the perfect will of God? One cannot pray the perfect will of God if one does not even believe in the Holy Spirit. (Romans 8: 26 – 28)

For example, if one is going to pray, then it is important for one to know what the will of God is in or for a particular situation. Often times we pray but it hinders God from truly moving, because they don't know His will.

Are we praying and calling on the names of God, because each name carries different results. God has a name for every situation and it is critical for us to use the name that applies to the situation at hand. If we want to be effective intercessors then we need to listen to what God is saying.

Are we praying the Word of God? Sadly, less than 20% of the Christians don't know the Word thus they don't know their rights. Most are just interested about getting a prophetic word about material items.
Let us recognize also that effective prayer does not mean hosting a Prayer Breakfast or a Prayer Conference and inviting the guest speaker to give a nice speech and talk about his books. If we don't help the poor and have mercy and compassion (Isaiah 58) our prayers will not be answered.

In order to achieve effective intercession there must be unity, regardless of one's class/status or denomination. Most want people to support them but when others who they deem unworthy of their presence, they will not support. If one wants results, one must be broken in humility before God!

To be effective in spiritual warfare prayer, one must be disciplined and willing to Fast. One cannot be walking in rebellion. A tree that is uprooted and replanted every month would die a slow death. Skipping from church to church will make one ineffective.

Intercession For Your Nation

Every person is required to pray if you want change. We must pray that God will reveal to us what we are really fighting against. Each of us is a watchman, and a watchman must stand in the gap. Standing in the gap means to bridge or repair what is broken. We must pray that God will deal with the epicenter of the problems and deal with the holes in the wall. We must be committed and disciplined! We must always remember that the word 'Intercession' in Hebrew is 'Paga' – which means to collide with, to encroach upon, to drive out, to strike up against, to be violent against' and so there is a measure of determination, effort and force in intercession.

As one who intercedes for his/her nation, one must:

Be confidential

Live holy – keep your conversations circumspect; and maintain openness and brokenness before God.

The Church was called to be a light for all and a pillar to the society.
When we pray, there must be some ground shaking. Effective intercession is not about our status, it is about our lifestyle. Hence, it is our duty to unite and begin praying if we want to live in peace and to have our children experience the peace; so that the will of God aligns with the earth. So that leaders make the right choices and not be deceived by the love of money; and that they will work in the interest of the poor and the suffering and not

for selfish gain. They must know that each one of them is accountable to God.

Moral And Spiritual Breakdown

The most dangerous things that can happen to a nation are moral and spiritual collapse.

Our nation has been heading in this direction for a long time and now it seems to have accelerated toward this dangerous place. No doctor can effectively treat any illness or issue unless they have properly diagnosed the patient. Thereafter, they can begin to apply to correct remedy to ensure restoration of good health.

Foundational Cracks

There are many within society today who are ignoring the obvious moral and spiritual breakdown taking place at every turn. Some believe that building roads and other tangible infrastructure, and the implementation of Artificial Intelligence (AI) throughout the entire societal framework, and the subtle mandating of vaccination will bring change to the society. However, when there is moral and spiritual breakdown, it means that the foundation is cracked and any builder will tell you that when the foundation cracks, no matter what you build on it, it is just a matter of time before everything comes falling down.

Leadership

Moral and spiritual breakdown starts from the top. When this happens, particularly in a Christian-based, God-centered society, the first "plan of action" given is always to secularize the society by rejecting God and the principles of God, pushing the Church into a corner – showing no respect to the Church by deeming it irrelevant, while promoting money and carnal, immoral activities as relevant to economic growth which is then deemed as the savior of the nation.

Identifying Moral and Spiritual Breakdown

Here a some of the things we will see when there is moral and spiritual breakdown in a society.

- ✓ Disorder.
- ✓ Lack of Value for Life
- ✓ Significant increase in levels of Crime and Violence
- ✓ Exploitation and Disappearance of Children
- ✓ Significant increase in rape
- ✓ Less marriages taking place while Divorce Rates increase
- ✓ Promotion of and Increases in Common Law Relationships and Promiscuity
- ✓ Significant increase in abortion rates and dramatic rise in the sale of dead embryos and body parts.
- ✓ Less desire to gather as the Church as the zeal for God slowly dies.

✓ Greed, sexual perversion, witchcraft, high levels of dishonor and lack of care for another become rampant in the society.

It is dangerous when God begins to give over a nation to their sinful practices, because will receive exactly what they ask for , including the repercussions that come along with it. Those repercussions include having leaders over the nation that will take away the nation's liberties.

Nations Are Born, Nations Die

Ecclesiastes 3: 1 – 2 says, *"To everything there is a season, a time for every purpose under heaven: A time to be born, and a time to die …"*

The decisions of every nation – morally and spiritually – will determine whether that nation lives or dies. Many nations in Europe and Asia are now dying. Surprisingly, many in the Caribbean have been and are still trying to be like those nations. When natural laws are broken there are always consequences. Likewise, the same goes for spiritual laws, and the impact for that is more far-reaching than anyone can imagine.

When the institution of Family begins to breakdown, that is the beginning of moral and spiritual collapse. Transformation and restoration of moral and spiritual collapse can only come through the Holy Spirit of God. It starts with repentance, prayer, fasting, prophesying – speaking the messages from God – not from man nor to please man, and spiritual cleansing according to Ezekiel

36 – so that God will give new hearts and new desires. Transformation happens from the inside out; and only God can bring transformation in a nation. Most want transformation by way of conforming to the blueprints of other nations. However, that would only propel greater moral and spiritual decline.

We have seen the political Ferris wheel in effect decade after decade in our nation with no effort to change. We continue to hear the big promises with little result. We hear of the fancy forecasts and plans to bring change for the better, and we must come to the realization that it is all talk and no action.

Sir Winston Churchill once said, "Politics is the ability to foretell what is going to happen tomorrow, next week, next month and next year. And to have the ability afterwards to explain why it didn't happen." This is what we see happening in our society.

Winston Churchill said, *"The one thing we have learned from history is that we don't learn from history."* However, I implore us all to learn from history and prepare for a great overturn.

The Threat of The Common-Law Relationship

"Flee sexual immorality. Every sin that a man does is outside the body, but he who commits sexual immorality sins against his own body. Or do you not know that your body is the temple of the Holy Spirit who is in you, whom

you have from God, and you are not your own ..." (1 Corinthians 6: 18 – 20)

If a nation is going achieve certain goals by 2030, then the crisis of Common-Law Relationships and children being born out-of-wedlock has to be addressed. Making efforts to achieve economic goals will not work unless we deal with this crisis. I know many within the society will quickly say abortion is the solution, but we cannot, as a society negate the value of life and the importance of teaching families the dangers of sex outside of marriage and the value of getting a solid education.

Having children out of wedlock will negatively affect those children's future – emotionally and spiritually. (Deuteronomy 23: 2) The institute of marriage must be respected, and its value held high. Marriage calls for real and deep commitment – common-law relationships do not. Children born out of wedlock brings a bastard curse on both individuals and nations. It opens the door to further poverty, crime, violence, and termination of purpose. It also causes that person to struggle with rejection, fear and opens doors to insecurity, incest and abortion. Furthermore, the fathers often reject their children which result from those relationships and those children grow without their fathers and the vicious cycle begins.

When we look through the communities – particularly (but not only) the inner-city communities, we see those problems manifesting in more than half of the families in these communities. A mother will live with a man for 20/30 years without being married to him; one woman will have 3 different fathers for her children; a man will live with one woman and have several in addition, and these issues have become a crisis that must be addressed. Ladies, if the man is not willing to make a commitment to you and solidify it with the ring then move on! You are worth the commitment.

The gender issues that politicians and lobbyists should be focusing on are promoting abstinence and teaching the value of maintaining your virginity for the one who values you. We should not be marketing contraceptives to people and especially to our youth -encouraging sex outside of marriage. Maintaining your virginity and sexual purity is more valuable than iPads, smartphones and pocket change. Exchanging your body for things from famous people is not worth it. Don't exchange sex for food, there are still institutions that will give you the help without requiring sexual favors from you.

You Become Who You Sleep With

1 Corinthians 6: 16 tells us: *"Or do you not know that he who is joined to a harlot is one body with her? For "the two," He says, "shall become one flesh." But he who is joined to the Lord is one spirit with Him."*

There is more to sex than being skin to skin. Sex is as much a spiritual mystery as it is a physical fact. In sex, two people become one, so if a man sleeps with a harlot, he becomes that and if you have sex with him, so do you. If a married person commits adultery and then goes home to sleep with his/her spouse, they have now caused that spouse to be polluted spiritually. That is why when most people are struggling in a relationship, they can tell that the other has strayed.

In Biblical times, (and it still happens today) if one is going to destroy a family or a nation they would do it through sex, by being yoked to the lineage of the ones they want to destroy. That is why you can't lie with everybody or marry just anyone – or "shack up" with anyone.

Action Needed

There needs to be a united effort to go through the community and educated them on these issues and Pastors need to bless the people and break the curse from those in or out of common-law relationships (instead of blessings animals). (Deuteronomy 28: 1-2 & 4).

- ✓ Have mass weddings for those in common-law relationships who desire to be married.

- ✓ Have discounts on wedding rings

- ✓ Banks should open Savings accounts for those newlyweds

- ✓ Christen/Re-Christen children who are born out-of-wedlock – regardless of their age.

The Revelations Of Psalm 8

Man was originally created higher than the angels and through Christ will be restored to that position. Romans 8: 14 – 17 says, *"For as many as are led by the Spirit of God, these are sons of God. For you did not receive the spirit of bondage again to fear, but you received the Spirit of adoption by whom we cry out, "Abba, Father." The Spirit Himself bears witness with our spirit that we are children of God, and if children, then heirs—heirs of God and joint heirs with Christ, if indeed we suffer with Him, that we may also be glorified together."*

We are the sons of God and everything that belongs to Christ belongs to us. We get all privileges from God through Jesus Christ. To live as sons of God, we must live in such a way that sin doesn't not dominate over us. We must allow the Holy Spirit to help us in that direction. God wants us to have His DNA, His image. If one has a child in the natural, but there is no evidence of DNA. Then that child does not belong to that person.

It is critical that those who carry the Father's DNA would have the:

- ✓ Vision of God
- ✓ Heart of God
- ✓ They Will Follow His Will and His Way
- ✓ Holiness
- ✓ Truth
- ✓ Walk in His Glory
- ✓ Supernatural Wisdom
- ✓ Victory
- ✓ Power
- ✓ Rule and Reign

- ✓ Likeness
- ✓ Walk In Love
- ✓ Love Souls

and as such, everything we do must be aligned with the Word of God. The Word of God is Jesus Christ; He is The Word.

Having your Father's DNA eliminates problems. We call Him Father only because of and through Jesus Christ. Every Child of God should know that if we have our Father's DNA we must not allow the enemy to confuse or trick us into believing that we are bastards. We are sons and daughters of the Almighty Father, not bastards; and we are no longer under the sin of the law anymore. There are certain privileges that we are entitled to, and we must walk in our privileges and authority.

Exalted With Christ

Every Christian should remember Ephesians 2: 4 – 7 *"But God, who is rich in mercy, because of His great love with which He loved us, even when we were dead in trespasses, made us alive together with Christ (by grace you have been saved), and raised us up together, and made us sit together in the heavenly places in Christ Jesus, that in the ages to come He might show the exceeding riches of His grace in His kindness toward us in Christ Jesus."*

Every believer is exalted with Christ. When Christ was resurrected from the tomb, we as believers were resurrected with Him as well; and symbolically, it also signifies that everything that is dead in our lives can be resurrected through Jesus Christ, including our health, our relationship with Him, and or your relationship with your spouse. Your finances, all the promises belong to us. It is time for rejection to go, self-pity, every curse, the bastard curse. Accepting Christ means everything becomes new in our lives. Christ 's promotion is our promotion.

Romans 6: 3 – 5 says, *"Or do you not know that as many of us as were baptized into Christ Jesus were baptized into His death? Therefore we were buried with Him through baptism into death, that just as Christ was raised from the dead by the glory of the Father, even so we also should walk in newness of life. For if we have been united together in the likeness of His death, certainly we also shall be in the likeness of His resurrection."*

His death and resurrection give us the richness if His grace, access to the Father, hope, restoration, newness, life, new covenant, forgiveness of sins, freedom, hope regardless of what.

Dominion

Psalm 8: 6 – 9 *"You have made him to have dominion over the works of Your hands; You have put all things under his feet, all sheep and oxen — even the beasts of the field, the birds of the air, and the fish of the sea that pass through the paths of the seas. O LORD, our Lord, How excellent is Your name in all the earth!"*

We have access to all resources, and they are there to serve us, not to enslave us; we have been given dominion over them. Furthermore, we are led by the Holy Spirit of God because we are sons of God. There are a lot of spirit out there but only One Holy Spirit. Many are led by different spirits. As sons we cannot operate without the Holy Spirit. We cannot walk as sons unless we have a relationship with the Father. God can only get His Glory in the earth through His children.

When our biological children do well in school, it is always an honor to the parents. When they do badly, it is a disappointment and let down. We are either vessels of honor or dishonor. God has crowned us as children with Glory and Honor (splendor, glory, distinction, prestige). There is no scientific discovery that can reduce the value of humans. There are many scientists trying to reduce the value of Human Being, some even trying to change the DNA of man. To being the image of others but God created us to be in the image of Him. All man needs to do is accept the Lord as Savior.

God Glorified Through Us

The message in Psalm 8 also speaks of one's gifts and talents from God and should be used for the service of God. God is to be glorified for making himself available to us. He even made the Heavenly Body for the benefit of Man. The Palms of David is a nature Psalms. It shows the littleness of physical man and the greatness of God. Although man is small in comparison to the Universe, he is nonetheless the pinnacle of creation and the object of God's watchful care.

Psalm 8 also reminds us that God is Sovereign, and that He is The Master. Infants utter praise unto Him every time they say "Abba' or "Hosanna". Mankind must understand that all glory belongs to the True and Living God – the Creator. There are many within the earth giving man greater praise than the Sovereign God, even their politicians. Some even promoting science over God who created everything. (Colossians 2: 6).

It is noteworthy that, 1 Corinthians 2: 31 reveals that true wisdom power and holiness can be only found in Jesus. Rejecting the Living God and making efforts to function in your own wisdom and ability will only bring failure. If God is the architect, creator, and designer then everyone is created by Him. The nature, the planet, air, life, and He put man in it to manage it with instructions. The only way we will be able to manage or survive is to follow his instruction. Then He will give us the knowledge and the understanding about how to care for the planet. We are responsible for the Universe. Everything we do against the true and living God brings consequences, which bring climate change. When man begin to walk in truth holiness and righteousness and not depend on their knowledge and intellect, then we will minimize most of the global problem taking place, which will include the reduction of diseases, pestilence and famine.

Chapter 7

COVID-19 AND THE CHURCH LOCKDOWN

The eyes of many within the Church globally are finally being opened to see the plan of the anti-Christ, but many are still under strong delusion because they refuse to listen to the truth. As 2 Thessalonians 2: 9 – 11 says, *"The coming of the lawless one is according to the working of Satan, with all power, signs, and lying wonders, and with all unrighteous deception among those who perish, because they did not receive the love of the truth, that they might be saved. And for this reason God will send them strong delusion, that they should believe the lie,"*

What we believe and who we believe are going to be critical for us in this season. This is a season where people will be required to pledge allegiance – whether Christ or anti-Christ. Those who are world-focused and materialistic will choose the anti-Christ. The mark of the beast is about allegiance in the end time. 666 is more than a number; it is about what the number represents. We are seeing most global leaders choosing the things of the anti-Christ rather than the things of Christ. If someone is putting his/her trust more in the vaccine than in Christ to heal and deliver us, while they justify closing the House of the Lord, then we will be seeing the numbers rise and new diseases coming to the fore.

Negatives and Positives

Since the COVID-19 pandemic started, we are seeing the revealing of many hearts, the falling away of members of the Body of Christ (Apostasy), anti-Christ laws being passed on the premise of scientific propaganda. Only the big businesses are making super-profits. Big Tech and Big Pharma are profiting while there is a major push to silent the Church – the true voices; and because of that, we may see the three (3) woes as told to us in Revelation, pour out upon the earth. That may include a global heatwave that may claim thousands of lives. We should watch the month of April and onward.

Rewards for Closing the Church

Let it be understood that the Church is God's business and when the business sector tries to sabotage the Church, we will see many devastating occurrences. There will be a wave of bankruptcy, more businesses will die; famine, shaking in politics, increased crime and violence, cosmic disruptions, earthquakes, increase in the occult as many will turn to evil. Selling the Lord for 30 pieces of silver always has tragic circumstances. There will be more hangings and suicides. The stock market will crash. Every secular institution must know that it is not the enemy that has given us the power to get wealth, but it is God. The world must know that when the economy of the Church fails, the World economy will also face devastation. Great men in the Bible – Solomon, Hezekiah, Pharaoh – built God's house.

Many have benefitted from the Church on a daily basis, the poor, the fatherless and the widow, salary of the priest, and those who serve in the House of God. The spiritual aspect of the nation is far more important than any other. In fact, God first created the economy before man. When man sins, it is thorns and thistles – man begins to labor with hard work when in the beginning everything was given to man freely. When we hinder people from worshipping God, where will the young converts be shepherded?

God's word specifically tells us that we are not to forsake the assembling of the brethren together. "Gathering" on the virtual platform is not accomplishing that instruction. In fact, the word virtual means that something is so in essence but not in actuality. It is not real.

Hebrews 10: 25, "Let us hold fast the confession of our hope without wavering, for He who promised is faithful. And let us consider one another in order to stir up love and good works, not forsaking the assembling of ourselves together, as is the manner of some, but exhorting one another, and so much the more as you see the Day approaching."

An "assembly" is "a group of people gathered together in one place for a common purpose." If governments lock down God's government in the earth, which is the Church, then He will also lock down their governments. So, there will be no meetings, no sessions, no law-making and no benefits for them. Everything will come to a standstill.

No Pastor can shepherd their flock without touching the sheep. A shepherd's primary responsibility is the safety and welfare of the flock and other duties include, flock welfare, protecting from predators, protecting the health of the sheep and shearing the flock that further includes the laying of hands, anointing their heads with oil, examining them for insects and diseases, and that cannot be done virtually. When the shepherd fails to do that, the flock will die as the sheep cannot survive without the shepherd. Whose hands will the blood be on?

The COVID-19 Fight

As the world grapples with fear as a result of the coronavirus, it is critical that nation leaders of the globe deal with the root cause of the problem. This must be a united effort by the various stakeholders - governments, the Church globally and civil society. We must be careful not to engage in discrimination of any kind in dealing with the Coronavirus pandemic (COVID-19). No nation must discriminate against any nation, regardless of the virus' origin, because this matter has the potential to escalate to a physical war and crashing economies. Furthermore, it has the potential for international sabotage.

Nations must abide by the Preamble of the UN Charter (1945). The blame game should not be played at any point as this will drive oil prices up to the detriment of many! Food prices have already gone through the roof. It will bring us even further into global famine and recession. There has to be a united effort, and leaders must be willing to learn about apocalyptic events and symbols – horses, seals and trumpets. What we can do as a nation – according to the books of Joel and Revelation – is unite and develop problem-solving strategies.

There needs to be tighter monitoring of the elites and the diplomats regarding the viruses as it stands today. They are the major carriers and their diplomatic immunity status does not help matters as they are excluded from certain checkpoints and other checks that the general public has to go through. Many politicians are already contaminated. While they may self-quarantine, others with which they come into contact are not.

There needs to be major fogging and cleaning of communities with cleaning agents that are not harmful to the general public. They must pay the community people to get involved in cleaning up their communities. This will help unemployment, increase morale and decrease the levels of lawlessness that has been occurring as a result of the community and national restrictions due to the pandemic.

Unless the current pandemic is a situation the millionaires and billionaires of the world want to see as their new normal, every single one of the world's wealthy must contribute significantly to aid and assist the nations to fight this common enemy. None is invincible and the need is dire and affects everyone – with or without wealth.

The WHO (World Health Organization) and Member states urgently need to assist poorer countries that will be affected by the coronavirus and other potential outbreaks. Countries such as Haiti, Puerto Rico and small

Caribbean Islands need urgent help. This is especially so for Haiti – it is more a dire need. We cannot fight any disaster that is classified under Climate Change without the wisdom and the knowledge of God. It is time that God is allowed a seat in the decision-making as a great deal of the advising taking place is done in a vacuum, fueled by fear and devoid of Divine Wisdom.

Is God Speaking Through The Virus

The world is in panic and fear because of the global Coronavirus pandemic. We are also seeing the locust plague affecting several regions, and by extension the entire globe, particularly the food supply for many nations. Prices are rapidly rising – almost out of control. Furthermore, the entertainment and sports industries are taking a hit and many economies are now saying we have entered a recession. The question is, could God be speaking to us through the virus? Many leaders throughout the globe have refused to listen to the voice of the Lord, abide by His word, and they have been mistreating the poor, the fatherless and the widow.

Climate Change

The Bible shows us that God speaks to people in many different ways – the wind, the whirlwind, storms, viruses, and plagues including locusts, as in the Book of Exodus. Furthermore, the Books of Joel and Revelation speak to us about horses, seals and trumpet. Different catastrophic events and happenings that would happen in the end time to get man's attention are what we now call "Climate Change." It is critical that the world embrace and experience a lifestyle change to have positive occurrences.

Lifestyle Change

Global leaders and the elite have created systems to put man in bondage. Today, as it was in the time of Moses, God has allowed ten plagues to hit the earth to tell the Pharaohs of the day, *"Let My People Go!"* God is dealing with the modern-day Pharaohs and what they call their gods.

The ten plagues then, were God's confrontation of their gods and belief systems, and symbolized fullness of the moral laws of God and the fullness of His justice and judgement. He also showed His power to save and deliver. Through the plagues, God was showing that the power of all prosperity came from Him. The belief in every god that the Egyptians served was confronted by the True and Living God through each plague, because each plague addressed a specific god's so-called span of "control." For example:

- ✓ *Heqet* was regarded as the goddess of fertility, water and renewal and was depicted in Egyptian culture as a frog or a woman with the head of a frog. Thus, God sent the plague of frogs as a reminder that He was the one in control and not *Heqet.*

- ✓ *Hapi* was the god of the Nile. God caused the water to turn into blood and no one could explain it or fix it but God – not Hapi; thus reminding every person Who was in absolute control.

- ✓ *Seth* was the god of the desert, foreign lands, thunderstorms, eclipses, and earthquakes and so the Lord hit Egypt with the desert locusts – found in Africa, the Middle East, and Asia. Egypt is the country that links Northeast Africa with the Middle East.

The Negatives and Positives of Viruses and Plagues

As the coronavirus fears rise, so will the demand for alternative healing and medicine. God will become the focus again. (Revelation 22, Revelation 47)

The Bible, in particular, the Books of Exodus, Daniel, Joel and Revelation will become the focus.

- ✓ New levels of unity will come to the fore.

- ✓ Families will be restored

- ✓ Wealth Transfer and fair distribution of the resources will begin

- ✓ New laws will pass regarding health and security.

- ✓ A change will take place in the global economy

✓ Famine, Bankruptcy, Shortage of Food and Medicine will take place – which is spoken of in Revelation and Daniel (the four horses) will take place. In fact, it has already begun.

✓ Changes will take place in the banking system in order to facilitate a cashless system. Interestingly, the W.H.O. recently made the announcement that money carries/spreads the virus.

✓ Farming will become a priority again as the first profession and nations that capitalize on that will rise to economic power.

✓ Oil and Communications industries will experience great demands and glitches in supply and trade.

✓ Homeschooling will be the order of the day.

✓ Entertainment and Sports industries will need to restructure

✓ Working from home will increase and commuting to work will reduce.

✓ We will see global changes where people will become more creative.

✓ Common sense, compassion and maturity will come to the fore again.

✓ Materialism will no longer be the number one focus, but people will begin to crave a deeper understanding of their purpose.

Is God Speaking Through The Scorching Heatwave

Revelation 16: 8 – 9, "Then the fourth angel poured out his bowl on the sun, and power was given to him to scorch men with fire. And men were scorched with great heat, and they blasphemed the name of God who has power over these plagues; and they did not repent and give Him glory."

Scorching Heat

Across Europe during summer 2022, the headlines read *"Scorching Heat...* as several "European countries experience record-breaking heat wave, Spain and Portugal have reported at least 1,169 heat-related deaths, according to each country's ministry of health.

At least 510 people died from heat-related issues in Spain between July 10 and July 18, 2022, the country's health ministry said. Of those deaths, 273 were recorded on Friday, officials said. Another 659 heat-related deaths were recorded in Portugal between July 7 and July 17, local officials said.

Thousands of firefighters were having trouble containing forest fires in France. In southern France, more than 14,000 people were forced to flee as fires spread to more than 27,180 acres of land."

"The high temperatures are coupled with a lack of water. U.N. officials say these unprecedented temperatures should be a wakeup call for government action."

If heads of governments are truly serious about dealing with climate change, then we cannot afford to ignore the cause of the scorching heat wave. Notice, the very word "scorching" is stated in the scripture. When we ignore the cause, then it will continue to cost us life, property, and more.

The Fourth Bowl

This scripture regarding the fourth angel and that fourth bowl outlines God's judgement on mankind in order to get them to repent. While the suffering will become intense, man still refuses to turn away from their wickedness.

Scorching heatwaves are part of the seven bowls spoken of in the Book of Revelation; and while the seven bowls have similarities to the seven trumpets, the seven trumpets were partial and constitute a call to repentance. However, the bowls are about the full manifestation of God's judgement. Hope will be dwindling for those who refuse to repent.

The first four bowls affect the environment:

- ✓ Loathsome sores
- ✓ Seas turning to blood
- ✓ Water turning to blood
- ✓ Heatwave

We have already seen loathsome sores happening via Monkeypox. We have seen where in Russia, the river Daldykan, which runs near the city, has turned blood red. The same has been reported about a canal in Nootdorp, the Netherlands; Bondi Beach in Australia; the Beirut River in Lebanon; a river in Zhejiang Province, China; rainfall in Sewanagala, Sri Lanka—all reported blood-red by reliable news outlets.

We are already seeing a shortage of fresh water and it is getting worse. Rivers globally are drying up and all that remains is dust.

The Happening Of The Last Three Bowls

The last three bowls include darkness and pain, the Euphrates drying up and the earth being utterly shaken.

The Euphrates may not seem to have much significance to someone far away, but the Euphrates is the last barrier to total destruction, clearing the way for the invasion from the east. That affects the entire world. (Revelation 9: 14 – 21) and will lead up to the Battle of Armageddon.

We have already seen, according to Revelation 9: 21, man-made plagues, war in the Ukraine and Russia, deception and sorceries - which is translated from the word *"pharmakia"* – meaning *"pharmacy"*, which generally describes the use of medicines, drugs or spells poisoning by drugs, incantations, charms and magic.

Military invasion is already happening. There is also the issue of the counterfeit trinity, false prophecies, lightnings, thunderstorms, record earthquakes globally happening now. It is judgement on the Babylonian system – the total collapse of cities and economies. Famine is imminent. There are deceptive miracles and the rising of the great harlot. (Revelation 17).

Deuteronomy 28: 22 says, "The Lord will strike you with consumption, with fever, with inflammation, with severe burning fever, with the sword, with scorching, and with mildew; they shall pursue you until you perish."

God will use all these things to get people to the point of repentance. We have seen some of the most anti-Christ laws being passed by nations globally. When the fear of God is no longer there, then woes will begin to take place. Droughts, fires, tribulations and diseases will break out as a result of disobedience to God.

Our farming is on the verge of global wipeout. Chaos, crises are increasing. Zechariah 14: 6 – 19 reminds us that nations that come against the apple of God's eye, will suffer great calamity. So, it is critical for nations to be mindful of the decisions they make.

Stand Faithful

For those who stand as God's people, we must encourage ourselves, because according to Isaiah 49: 10, He will protect us as we stay faithful.

Chapter 8

CHRISTIANS, COVID AND THE VACCINE

There Is a crisis brewing globally regarding Christians and the forcing of the vaccine. Christians are now being given the ultimatum that they must take both the flu vaccine as well as the vaccine for COVID-19 and also submitting to a COVID-19 Test. They are using the term mandatory, and if not they will be without a job. It has already begun. Thousands of Christians are now losing their jobs. We have seen religious rights being ignored by men. This is a developing crisis in the Body of Christ and many Church leaders are ignoring this Crisis. It is getting worse and it will also impact the spiritual and financial environment within the church.

As the Body of Christ, we have been focusing on the wrong areas. I believe that by January 2022, there is going to be a global move to mandatory vaccination. A vaccine should never be forced. A person's religious right should not be violated by mandatory vaccines. Furthermore, Christians will need to make a choice as one wrong move can destroy their future. It is critical for the Church to begin putting plans in place to deal with the fallout that will be taking place – which includes job loss. Furthermore, the family and the Church will be affected. The Real Estate Industry will be directly affected.

It is a shame that there are alternatives to the vaccine that will deal with the COVID-19, but the authorities have refused to endorse or validate the remedy. For example, Revelation 22, Ezekiel 47: 12, and Genesis 2: 9 clearly offer to us the solutions for the healing of the nations. Christians also have the Blood of Jesus and the gift of Healing as resources to bring the healing to the nations.

Solutions

Pastors need to quickly begin teaching the people about the books of Ezekiel, Daniel and Revelation, because it will hep the people to understand the Anti-Christ Spirit. They also need to have a plan in place like the Book of Act, to help Christians that will be persecuted because of their decision against taking the vaccine. By taking the vaccine, we may see the results of Revelation 16: 1 – 2 manifest – sores and skin disease and more will breakout upon those who take that vaccine as a sign of judgement upon those who take it, as the vaccine may very well be the mark of the beast. It is said that with the nano particles in the vaccine, man will become like human antennas which will also be used for marketing and geo-marketing, and they will also contain important health information which will be in the hands of the authorities under the Anti-Christ agenda. So, when they know all your details and health information, then things become dangerous.

It is interesting that the patent for the vaccine carries the number "060606" (666). The activities of the individual will be monitored, and each person will be rewarded with cryptocurrency. A **cryptocurrency** is a digital or virtual currency that is secured by cryptography, which makes it nearly impossible to counterfeit or double-spend.

Every Christian needs to understand that we belong to The Most High God. We were created in His image, and each of our DNA is unique to each one of us. Whatever they would inject is to unlock and decode each person's unique DNA information and manipulate and redesign our genetic makeup for their purpose.

When the is a patent for a product, then whoever holds the patent owns it and is entitled to anything that product becomes a part of – which means, if they own the patent, they own you.

What Should Christians Do

The main fact that Christians have started to lose their jobs based on their refusal to take the vaccine or be tested for COVID-19, is an indication that they need to start owning their own business quickly! They cannot trust the political or business sectors to have our best interest at heart; we have to trust God. Remember this, anything genetically modified has an owner.

God will use the Exodus of Christians that is ahead, to destroy the Babylonian system that currently exists. (Revelation 18: 4)

God is about to deal with the merchants, the businesses and the rich, who believe they can move God out of the business and that they have the right to destroy the population. When they try to force Christians out because they refuse to take the vaccine and other medication that go against the Christian beliefs, there will be a crash in the marketplace.

This is a wakeup call for every Christian and we must open our eyes, listen to the voice of the Lord and obey Him!

Covid-19 Protocols Will Destroy The Travel Industry

Some of the new travel bans and travel protocols that have been and continue to be imposed will create a serious, negative impact on the travel industry globally, particularly the airline industry.

It is critical for decision-makers to think clearly about the decisions they are making. Many of these decisions regarding masks, screening imposition of COVID tests, health passports, vaccines, as well as tracking and surveillance, are not necessarily for the purpose of the COVID-19 pandemic. It would seem as if the COVID-19 pandemic situation is the platform for rolling out many of these plans currently being executed.

While many talk about "conspiracy theories" it is frightening that Revelation 13 outlines much of what is being implemented today. We can't buy or sell unless we comply. Many of the new COVID protocols are being rolled out particularly in poorer countries, who are being held at ransom, so-to-speak, if they do not comply.

If decision-makers were putting enough effort in creating the solutions for the COVID-19 the way they are pushing for vaccines and other testing, the problem would have already been solved. Since the rollout of vaccines, we are seeing stocks jump, particularly in the travel industry as if many think the problem is solved by the vaccines. So, it pushes of stocks. However, if these decisions are not revisited quickly, they are going to destroy the travel industry. Less people will be interested in travelling – especially the poor. The cost to travel has become so expensive; that coupled with the new protocols will drive the industry into the ground. It will also affect the following:

- ✓ Tourist industries – particularly in poorer countries
- ✓ Bi-lateral and Multi-lateral Agreements among nations
- ✓ Businesses – particularly small businesses
- ✓ Unemployment Levels (increase)
- ✓ Production Levels in Manufacturing
- ✓ Real Estate

The decisions made will also affect the Agricultural and Food-related industries as well as the fuel industry. Furthermore, plazas will lockdown and be empty, five-star hotels will be closed, airports, car rental companies and car marts will be negatively affected; and in addition to this, so will the sports and entertainment industries. Ultimately, import, exports, The fallout will also bring an economic depression as the globe continues to ignore God's principles for problem-solving.

While these issues may open new markets and opportunities for the rich to travel o their private jets, it may also open the door for human rights violations to make vaccines mandatory for pilots. That is a no-no.

Every leader – whether in a nation or an organization – has the responsibility to seek Divine Help to address this problem, rather than further demolish the economies and bring the globe into further depression.

In order to balance business and daily life while saving lives, it is critical to see things beyond the scientific. It is therefore critical for nations to bring into the equation, persons from different sectors and perspectives along with Divine help to garner solutions in these times. We must also ensure that the pandemic does not become a profit-making venture at the lives of others, as ever life – every soul – is valuable to God. What a man sows, he shall in fact reap.

Every country has the right to create their own solutions and not to follow a script. Remember, there are 193 nations that are each sovereign and must be allowed to function as such, regarding the decisions their governments make for their people. Nations need to stop hanging on to and accepting every single word coming from scientists, billionaires and so-called experts only with and taking what they say as the only solution. Furthermore, in our efforts to reduce the spread of COVID-19 on airlines and other modes of transportation, we should not only look at the potential for profit-making, we should be focused mainly on servicing, maintenance and sanitization of the vehicles and equipment within the fleet and within the hotel industry, reducing the load sizes (in the same way they did for small businesses and churches). If we really want change, then there can be no double standards in protocol.

In addition to this, in an effort to stop the spread among flight attendants in the airline industry, then airlines will need to hire more attendants, increase the salaries and insurance, while having shorter hours for flight attendants, instead of putting the pressure on a few.

Chapter 9

DEALING WITH A VIRUS-LED ECONOMY

Lockdowns were everywhere. Fear, shortages, and riots in some places. In the midst of that, there are some serious questions that should be answered. No one should use the status of the world today as a political platform because it will not be an easy road ahead.

I have been warning for many years – in articles, through books and prophecies – which can be found in the Gleaner's archives. While the Gleaner may be quarantining my articles recently, if we are not willing to deal with or face the truth, then how are we going to find the solutions? Are we willing to listen? Our "expert" advisors are so arrogant that they refuse to listen. Are we prepared to deal with the next phase of the coronavirus and how it will impact the economy – especially investors! I know may in the business community don't usually want to hear the truth because they believe it will negatively impact the economy. But if fear and panic on one issue can negatively impact the economy, then the economy was built on sand.

Causes

Not even the WHO (World Health Organization is able to tell us how the virus operates. The CDC (Center for Disease Control) worked frantically, while countries went into lockdown mode one-by-one as if to follow some unwritten protocol – almost as if they are following each other. So, if each country is sovereign, and each has an independent health system, where was the creativity in dealing with the virus?

If there are so many people getting infected, then this disease must be airborne. If that is so, then what is the purpose of "social distancing"? We should be touching and agreeing for Divine intervention to spare our economy, and for the eradication of the viruses and the plagues. Nations should be calling prayer and fasting to ask God to send a West wind to remove the East wind of death and destruction. Instead of a lockdown, shouldn't the people get outside of the building for sunlight and air to recover faster?   Does anyone know what the incubation period of this disease? Can this virus affect vegetables and other foods and fruits? Is this disease biological in nature?   Should we be boiling our vegetables for a certain period of time to ensure safety? Is this disease affecting animals? Is animal meat safe for consumption? Should we be boiling our foods and meat for 10 minutes at least in order to get rid of the pathogens?

Seeking Divine Intervention

Unless global leaders get all stakeholders at the table and seek Divine intervention, then we are on the course of greater calamity regarding the economy. God created the economy before He created man. To that end, isn't God qualified to instruct nations on what to do in this crisis? If we refuse to listen, then a new market will be created.

- ✓ Building Permits and Capacity will be affected

- ✓ Forced Vaccinations and Population Control will take place

- ✓ Counterfeit vaccines and tests that will give inaccurate results

- ✓ Famine and recession will accelerate

- ✓ Food and drinkable water shortage will happen

- ✓ Expansion of the military number to curtail the movements of the people and avoid riots

Default in Loan Payments to countries like China for example, opens the door for China to own the countries and control the Global Economy.

For churches that believe it is okay to be complacent now and depend solely on online broadcasts, they will soon begin to charge where it was once free of charge. Furthermore, they will be censored. In fact, it has already begun. We should never forsake the assembling of the brethren together.

- ✓ Every nation's number one priority should be farming – for the sake of survival. It is not business as usual.

✓ Oil prices must be drastically reduced.

Furthermore,

✓ Doesn't the church qualify for a stimulus package since they too are required to pay mortgage and staff?

✓ How sure are we that those who have received the vaccine for the coronavirus administered by some countries will not relapse?

✓ Isn't it time for us to focus on Revelation 22: 2 and Ezekiel 47: 1 – 12 regarding Divine cure?

It is time for global leaders to unite and stop pointing fingers – so we can prevent a global recession.

Not Time To Open The Economy

There is a debate concerning whether or not we should open the economy now. There is division on this issue, and as President Trump declares the US Economy open, it is expected that many countries will follow the lead of the United States of America.

I believe we are in a time where God is speaking to global leaders that the way they do business and the way we lead can no longer work as we move forward. We must change the way we operate in order to minimize losses or else create further spread of the virus and other potential plagues.

We must learn from Noah. The flood lasted about 150 days, however, before Noah ventured out he sent two birds ahead – a dove and a raven. The raven is a scavenger, so it feeds on dead flesh. The dove is not, but instead, gravitates toward life. When the raven did not return but the dove did, Noah knew that the raven had found dead flesh, so it was not safe to venture out. However, when the dove returned with the olive branch in its beak, he knew that new life was springing up and that branch symbolized fertility.

New Covenant

I felt that before the economy is reopened, the nation first needed to make a new covenant with God as Noah did, with repentance and thanksgiving in order to avert a major recession in the nation. We must now change our focus from greed to benevolence. We could use the remainder of April and the month of May as a time of prayer and reflection and open the economy in June. It will also be the time of Pentecost, where God will pour out His Spirit to deal with the greater problems ahead and the other pandemics that are slated to happen – skin and eye diseases that will break out.

The Danger of Opening Too Soon

There will be serious problems that will affect the airline industry. So, the airline industry as well as others in the transportation industry, will need to properly service and sanitize airplanes, cars, buses ships and all methods of public transportation. This will minimize the spreading of the disease locally and globally. Going forward there will need to be proper and regular maintenance, in order to prevent catastrophe and sabotage. It would also go a far way in protecting staff and passengers.

Attacks on the more vulnerable countries – those nations that suffered most during the pandemic. There needs to be time for Rest, Regrouping and Refocus. This will allow all involved to be better able to assess, evaluate, fortify and protect the communication systems, bridges, water supply systems, ports and so on. Furthermore, the hurricane season is ahead and there needs to be adequate attention given to stockpiling, logistics and preparation.

Apocalyptic Events

It is critical for nation-leaders to understand the Times and Seasons and the relevance of the four horses and horsemen, particularly regarding The **Pale Horse** and its rider. The Pale Horse is a symbol of disease, death, and devastation that will break out and brings with it issues such as the shortage of medication, ocean-related problems and the death of a significantly large number of fishes.

We must also prepare for global oil shortage and high oil prices, in addition to serious problems in Real Estate.

A nation that does not prepare will suffer greater problems ahead. It is critical that we begin to build with God. We must ensure that we don't repeat our mistakes and avoid unnecessary crises.

The other 3 symbols of the Horses are also critical to our decision-making going forward.

The White Horse symbolizes international power and politics, more so in the form of military conquest and global deception. Many countries will be conquered through loans that they are borrowing from other countries. Warning for countries that keep borrowing loans. Many loans will be default and many countries will find themselves in trouble.

The Red Horse symbolizes civil war and strife – and this speaks for itself.

The Black Horse symbolizes economic disruption. Inflation is imminent and many things will become scarce. There will be labor problems, low wages and rampant starvation.

Ultimately, all indications tell us that we must not seek to move forward at any level without putting God first.

Recession Brings New Opportunities

In the marketplace today, there is great fear of a pending recession, and it is causing global anxiety attacks. Many are calling for the replacement of the dollar, as the reserve currency. Some say there is going to be worldwide economic collapse/recession.

Any economic system built without the principles of God will always be unstable. God has a principle and a blueprint for each nation must operate regarding how they are to operate. It doesn't make sense to debate which system is better – whether socialism or capitalism. Both are flawed and both have failed the people.

Best System of Government

Socialism is mainly focused on secularism – a system without God – and God is replaced with the word "State". Psalm 127: 1 reminds us that, "Unless the Lord builds the house, they labor in vain who build it; Unless the Lord guards the city, The watchman stays awake in vain." Once God is removed from the society, it becomes a Godless society.

Capitalism has also failed because of greed and corruption, and we have seen more countries which are deemed capitalists, fail to protect the poor. More laws are being passed to marginalize the poor. While capitalism supports private ownership – being free to work, trade and own land – we have seen over the years, some of the greatest transfers of wealth from the poor to the rich, including bailouts for the wealthy while the poor are forced to live on the streets.

All things being considered therefore, the best system of government and economy would then be the Theocratic system of government with One Who champions for the poor – God! He has a welfare system for the poor. It is called the Law of Gleaning, which would take care of the poor who have fallen on hard times. It supports self-reliance, debt freedom, debt forgiveness and restoration of property after a specified number of years. It also supports big businesses writing off the debts of smaller business, and the debts of poorer nations being written off by the wealthier ones. All this teaches us that riches and wealth are gifts given by God to be extended to others in need.

When we see capitalist countries begin to remove systems that would benefit the poor likewise, socialist countries are removing anything that mentions God at any level, then we are certainly heading for a recession.

Theocracy also supports private ownership – where trade can take place and family is the first priority. It operates with Grace, Mercy and Compassion.

Recession And Opportunities

The righteous should never fear recession, it raises up new millionaire and gives nations new direction, new advisors and transfers wealth into the right hands.

Recession has the potential to:

Show Who is really in charge of the economy – that it is and it provides major opportunities and support for the poor.

Allows other nations that are willing to apply Biblical Principles to begin to rise in and to power. Those who have food and water.

Farming will become the number one priority. People will begin to create new opportunities for survival. For example, gold, land acquisition, real property and the rental business, and franchising will all be the focus instead of the stock market. Instead of the banks, more private entities will come to the fore to give people an alternative for loans at a lower interest rate.

Allow for less manipulation, and as a result, a new market environment will emerge, that will change the way business will be done. The Barter System may once again emerge.

Faith and Trust in God will be restored, and nations and businesses will begin to pray again for solutions. A new breed of managers and leaders will emerge – those who will not depend on their academic qualifications to bring success but will instead trust God to do sol

The Church will (also) get back to their core mandate of dealing with the total man. There will be a fair distribution and the haves will help the have nots – like the Acts Church, where those who have more than one will willingly give to those who have none. (Acts 2: 42; Acts 4: 32 – 37)

We should not fear recession, because it acts as a societal and national reset, bringing things back to basics for a fresher, fairer start.

Chapter 10

DESTROYING HUMANITY IN THE NAME OF SCIENCE

There is a war going on. Humanity is being destroyed in the name of Science by way of manipulation, greed and control. Scientists have been trying to change everything that God originally created. First, it began with changing the definition, structure and role of family as God ordained it, then they sought to facilitate that by introducing the change to genders – increasing it from two to over one hundred. They are increasing efforts to remove the patriarchal aspect of (and significance in) the family – changing men into women and, women into men to show the men that they can be better men than the original. Now, they have launched the modification of man's DNA under the guise of helping the human race.

In an article from ScienceMag.org on April 15, 2021 entitled, "**Lab-Grown Embryos Mix Human And Monkey Cells For The First Time**" it is stated, "*By slipping human stem cells into the embryos of other animals, we might someday grow new organs for people with faltering hearts or kidneys. In a step toward that goal, researchers have created the first embryos with a mixture of human and monkey cells. These chimeras could help scientists hone techniques for growing human tissue in species better suited for transplants, such as pigs.*"

The destruction of agriculture, (food and livestock), aquaculture (sea food/life) under the guise of sustaining life for mankind, are also part of their arsenal. They are developing lab grown meats, fruits, vegetables, starches and "seafood" in their efforts to "produce" more food for global consumption. Recognize that modification of God's creation will cause death and destruction. We are already seeing what they call climate change taking place. However, the reason these things are happening to us in the first place is as a result of their harmful actions and lifestyles. Sin and rebellion against God, and the modification of His creation are the major causes of sickness and disease globally.

Every scientist and investor need to read and understand Psalm 2 and Psalm 8.

God created the body to repair itself. The very things to sustain our health – food, environment, air everything – was perfect, and God gave man the opportunity to manage it all and be good stewards, but man never sought God on how to maintain it all – and we see the result of that today.

The Bible tells us in Daniel 12: 4 *"But you, Daniel, shut up the words, and seal the book until the time of the end; many shall run to and fro, and knowledge shall increase."*

Yet while the Bible speaks of knowledge increasing in the end time, it is not about increasing in efforts to replace God and all He has created/done, it is to increase in the knowledge and things of God – giving man a greater revelation of Who He is, while unlocking some mysteries that will benefit the human race.

Surprisingly, since the pandemic started, we have seen "Big Tech" companies trying to function like gods. When we realize that such companies can silence the head of a nation, then we must recognize that their reach and influence is more than meets the eye.

Clearly, the battle we are facing with scientists is Population Reduction through the elimination of a large portion of the population, restricting the Good News of Jesus to mankind. The activities taking place in outer space and the continued promotion of UFOs (Unidentified Flying Objects) may be preparation of things to come. We should also be vigilant of the livestock and other animals. Soon many of them might become stark-staring mad as a result of the testing and experiments being done to them.

Every scientist should know that anything man creates without God's blessing will not last. God's blessing is what makes the difference. When He created the earth, everything within it as well as the heavenly bodies, He blessed them all, and that blessing was the seal of approval and authenticity!

The question is, with all that they are "creating" do they have God's blessing? Furthermore, are we ready for a communication black out?

Scientists And Their Artificial Sun

Several articles from well-known and highly regarded sources have stated that scientists in China have "created" an artificial sun, while scientists in the United States have started their endeavor to block the real sun.

The South China Morning Post, in an article by Marsha Borak, dated November 27, 2019 stated that "China's completed 'artificial sun' to start operation in 2020. China's HL-2M nuclear fusion device burns with the power of 13 suns."

Intelligent Living, in an article dated January 20, 2020, by Luana Steffen, stated, "China built an artificial sun to achieve nuclear fusion energy." It further stated, "China's artificial sun is a nuclear fusion device that produces energy similar to the reactions that take place at the sun's core. Chinese scientists plan to start operations on the device soon. If successful, scientists could achieve the ultimate goal of cheap, clean, near-limitless, nuclear fusion energy."

Cosmic Interference

From the beginning of time, the Book of Genesis, man under the guise of Science, has been attempting to interfere with God's Creation. In Genesis 11, we where Nimrod and the city of Babylon were trying to destroy God's Creation. Some refuse to worship God but prefer to worship the zodiac and other planetary bodies. Their actions have caused sicknesses – plagues and diseases, and have opened the proverbial door, for more devastating plagues to enter.

Prophetically, the sun symbolizes the Light of God, the Truth and the Glory of God. Naturally-speaking, the Sun affords mankind vitamin D, and supports the growth of foods, plants and all of nature. The sun eliminates disease and stimulates the pineal gland which is located at the base of the brain and produces as well as regulates hormones, including melatonin, which promotes good sleep.

Seasons And Our Health

Has the thought ever occurred to you that we become ill so frequently because we spend so much time in the air conditioning and so little time in the sun? God also created different seasons, that produce different fruits to sustain mankind and its health; so certain fruits come in certain seasons. For example, a peach is a summer fruit – it bears mainly in the summer. In the summer, the heat of the sun intensifies. Could it be that God allowed the peach to be a summer fruit because He created it with nutrients and other things with all that is needed to protect our skin from absorbing too much sun and prevent skin (or other) cancers? It is said that the peach may aid digestion, improve heart health, protect your skin prevent certain types of cancer, and reduce allergy symptoms. Interestingly, allergy season runs from February into June.

Environmental Alignment

When God made the covenant with man and the earth, in Genesis 8, He declared six (6) seasons, and they all had sot do with proper alignment of the environment, growth and development.

God gave us free air to breathe and because of man's actions and sin against the earth, we are now subject to wearing masks which means that we are breathing in the carbon-dioxide we breathe out to sustain the trees that in turn give us the oxygen we need to breathe and live.

Lack of sunlight carries many disadvantages to mankind and the earth, including weight gain, weak bones, depression, skin problems, stress and much more. The sun helps our immune system. The W. H.O. has stated that each person needs 5 – 15 minutes of sunlight at least twice weekly. The sun also positively impacts our blood pressure.

Sun-Blocking

So, when we interfere with the sun – whether blocking it out or creating false one – we are interfering also with the seasons. We are creating grievous problems for ourselves.

Therefore, when scientists from highly esteemed institutions such as those at Harvard make "...plans to tackle climate change through geoengineering by blocking out the sun .... artificially reflecting sunlight..." not only are they engaging in activities that can prove detrimental the earth and our existence, but it is an attempt to control some things over which they have not Divine authority to control.

God created the climate perfectly. It is the sin of man - greed, pride – which negatively affects our environment and propels what they deem climate change. So, in order to correct that situation, 2 Chronicles 7: 13 – 14 and Hebrews 11 must come in to play. Prayer, Repentance and God's Word in action must be the order of the day.

Mammon And Mad Scientists

We have seen many international happenings. Nations are shaking, and many in positions of influence are attempting to fix the problem without getting to the root of the situation. This creates more deception and oppression. The number one element creating much of the global problems being faced is Mammon.

Mammon

Jesus teaches that mammon demands a person's heart and service and that those who persist in pursuing mammon cannot do any service to God, because mammon itself is a god, and many are losing sight of their true purpose because of it.

Mammon causes people to be deceived by having them gain prosperity through deception, dishonesty murder (including death to the masses), selfishness and fame/popularity. Their decisions are driven by selfishness and greed.

The Church

Mammon has been manifesting in the Church as many have shifted their focus from laying up treasures in heaven to gathering and storing treasures on earth. So, they are no longer fulfilling the command of Jesus; their focus is on financial profit-making. (Matthew 6: 24, Luke 16, 9 – 13, Luke 12: 16)

Mad Scientists

The COVID-19 pandemic has shown us that the world's scientists have gone mad. When scientists refuse to abide by Spiritual laws, then they create more problems. We are seeing their limitations on the public platform and most only give advice that would cause further deaths. Scientists are making decisions that will undoubtedly destroy the future for our children, as well as our environment and our seniors. This will cause further catastrophe and open the door for more of the biblical plagues we are already seeing today. Take a moment to compare what is written in the Book of Exodus, to our circumstances today. It was a rebuke by God to the Pharaohs of the day as a result of their actions. Unless there is an immediate cessation of their activities - including interference with the climate and environment, we are about to see the following take place that will create more pandemics and lockdowns, recession and other economic disasters. There will be Skin Diseases of every kind as well as Tumors, Blisters, Boils, Running Sores, Scabs, Itching, Confusion, Plagues, Consumption, Fever, Inflammation with burning Fever, Environmental Disasters, Scorching and Mildew; and some of these will be accompanied by Headaches, Madness and Blindness. Deuteronomy 28: 27 and Exodus 9: 8 – 12, speak of the incurable afflictions.

It is critical also, for global governments, businesspeople, scientists and the Church, to understand that when man violates God's original blueprint for mankind and the earth for the sake of profit, we are paving the way for future catastrophic events and more lockdowns.

God created six seasons, which are mentioned in Genesis 8: 22, and when scientists interfere with these seasons, it will create sever challenges for us all going forward. Trying to create vaccines or artificial intelligence for the masses to employ is not the solution. We are already contaminating our oceans and corrupting our water supply and destroying marine life ultimately affecting human life negatively.

When man tries to change God's seasons to suit himself, then the door is open for Diseases, Dust Storms, and Optical and Respiratory Issues.

They will come with the vaccines for these issues solely for making money not our health.

2030 Goals

With the promotion of the Global 2030 Agenda in achieving the Sustainable Development Goals, it is critical that every stakeholder take responsibility to create a better environment and achieve each goal outlined. We have already been delayed because of the pandemic, and it is critical that each person evaluates himself in terms of his actions in creating a better world. There needs to be an independent organization to police the actions of different member states/countries and scientists in their efforts toward a better world.

We must all come to the understanding that when we interfere with the flow and function of the original creation, then we open the door to desolation, and create greater negative impact on the poor and vulnerable, making the way for starvation and utter despair.

Chapter 11

CAN LIGHT AND DARKNESS CO-EXIST?

God created everything for a purpose. They will last when it is used for the purpose God created it for. Every part of our body was created to function in a particular way an orderly form. Once the body part does not function the way it is created to function, then we'll have hell problem. When Man tries to change or modify the purpose of God's creation, then we'll have problems. That is why we what you call climate change, as man trying to adjust the climate of the original way of creation. Man have created everything fake now, including food, temperature, the sun, the moon. It may sound strange, but it is true.

The first thing God did when He created the universe, was to separate light from darkness. (Genesis 1: 4). This is the key example which reveals the fact that light and darkness cannot co-exist. So, when man attempts to duplicate or modify the original, then we will have chaos and death.

The Night and Day Rotation

Scientists have been attempting over the years to have light and darkness to co-exist, but it has not and will not work. There is no way night and day can appear together. The change between day and night is caused by the rotation of the earth on its axis. Furthermore, daylight hours are affected by the tilt of the earth's axis while it revolves around the sun. Night occurs when the sun tilts to the other side of the earth. The "Sun" represents the light of God, His Truth, and the Glory of God. It also symbolizes Jesus Christ the Savior, and what that says is that as you turn and yield to Him, you will receive Light, Life, Truth and His Glory.

In Psalm 19: 6, David described the rotation of the earth from the viewpoint of a man from the earth and he is not teaching that the sun revolves around the earth. By comparison we use the word like sunrise and sunset to inscribe earth rotation when technically the sun does neither.

The Darkness

When there is darkness, it means that part of the earth is not facing the sun. Likewise, many are turning away from Jesus Christ, Who is the Son, it means they are not facing the Son, and as such are falling into darkness.

In darkness, the space and everything around looks black because there is no source of light nearby like the sun, and it is the same those who turn away from the Son – Jesus Christ. When they do, they are in darkness.

In the same way the children of light because they turned to the Son, they became a reflection of His radiant light. So, when the physical night takes place, they are always the light. Interestingly, that those that are in Darkness

126

benefit from us as children of Light. So, if there is a Light out, it would not affect us, but those who are not able to see.

The rapture of the Children of Light – The Church – will bring the earth into total Darkness literally and spiritually, so it will be total chaos. We can also just imagine when there is a total electrical block out and there is no light like flashlight and any other light, just imagine when the Children of Light are taken out, it will be more difficult at that time for people to move about.

The Moon, The Church

The Moon reflects the Sun, and the moon represents the Church

The Moon symbolizes the Church which reigns in the night season, and the Moon also reflects The Light of God. The Moon has to depend on the Sun. So, when the Moon turns into Blood, it symbolizes the Persecuted Church. Joel 2: 31 and Acts 2: 20. We must also look at Revelation 6: 11-13. It speaks about the Blood Moon, which symbolizes the spiritual and physical problems and the opening of the Seals.

The Moon also speaks to us about times and seasons. It speaks to us about harvest. The Moon is very important prophetically in the End Time, even the farmer uses the Moon to plant and to reap. The Moon also speaks of the economy, so when they persecute the Church, they are destroying their own harvest and economy. The success of the economy is the success of God's Church in the earth. When many countries trying to pass laws to curtail the Church, they are destroying their own harvest.

So, God's Children are the salt and the Light in the earth and if we try to get all Christians out of the organizations because of what they believe, will cause famine, death, lack, crime and violence will increase and there will be no light to suppress the darkness. With all the countries that are trying to purge Christianity, countries like communist countries and Muslim countries, what do we think would happen to those countries? Even fertility is affected by the Moon. Joel 2: 31 says *"The sun shall be turned into darkness, and the moon into blood, before the coming of the great and awesome day of the Lord,"* which means we will also see many anti-Christ laws pass to force Christians to be conformed to darkness, which is sin, lies and deception.

Tolerance Plan

What the enemy want is for Christians to tolerate darkness, the enemy wants a co-existence of Light and Darkness, but based on Scripture and God's design, it cannot be a co-exist of Light and Darkness because God divided Light and Darkness from the very beginning. It is not even scientific for light and darkness to co-exist at the same time. This is similar to the concept of being unequally yoked; saved and unsaved, as both light and darkness have two different desires. So, if an unsaved and a saved person marries or get into any form of covenant, eventually one will seek for Church and one seek for Club, one will seek for righteousness and one seek for sin. See Genesis 1:18, and 2 Corinthians 6: 14 says *"Do not be unequally yoked together with unbelievers. For what fellowship has righteousness with lawlessness? And what communion has light with darkness?"*

Matthew 24: 29 – 30 says *"Immediately after the tribulation of those days the sun will be darkened, and the moon will not give its light, the stars will fall down from heaven, and the powers of the heavens will be shaken." "Then the sign of the Son of Man will appear in heaven, and then all the Tribes of the earth will mourn, and they will see the Son of Man coming on the clouds of heaven with power and great glory."*

The Meaning of the Fallen Star

The star symbolizes descendants, and also symbolizes Jesus Christ. There are many debates about whether or not Christians will be in the Tribulation period. Based on the scripture, Christians will be part of the Tribulation and during this time, the sun will be darkened. This means that Christians will be around in the Tribulation, but the Church will already be raptured. The Holy Spirit will begin to restrain and there will be less light, less direction within the earth. A fallen star symbolizes the Apostate Church.
So, when the star falls from heaven, we will see the arrival of the Apostate Church in the earth; it has already begun.

The Apostate Church will substitute darkness for light and fully embrace all the things of darkness. The Apostate

Church will also be blinded, so they will not see what the Lord is doing, know, nor will they be able to understand how the Lord will move. They will join with the anti-Christ to persecute the true Church. Furthermore, they will not have any solutions; they will stumble in the darkness. they will be a mockery within the earth. They will be agents of Satan – the Marketing and Public Relations team for the things of darkness. The "solutions" that will come from darkness, will bring destruction into the earth. A person in darkness, will have no problem to kill, steal and destroy. Those in darkness see light as boring, foolish, and a threat, because darkness is afraid to be exposed. It will be interesting to see what will take place in the End Times, particularly in the marketplace, and the political sector – it will be chaos.

As children of Light, we need to continue impacting the globe positively. Our lives must be so bright that darkness is expelled wherever we go. Light must also bring growth, peace, joy, love, and transformation. Only Light can bring order within the globe.

It is important for us to know that whenever we see countries and nations where crime and violence increases, it means that there is darkness ruling.

Moon Turns into Blood

It is critical for us spiritually and physically to observe the signs of times, especially the Moon. Remember the Moon speaks to us about Church and the Seasons to better understand how to prepare for the season, to watch the laws that are changing, as most leaders globally will be ruling by decree, which is the system of the ant-Christ. It will be about allegiance; it is critical to see who will pledge allegiance to whom.

There are many things that will be imposed upon the globe under the disguise of economics and security reasons. Many leaders will only make decisions based on gold and silver. Money will be their god, but during turmoil in the End Time, we will see the manifestation of Malachi 4: 2 – global healing and restoration of God's people will take place. We will see the anointing of Elijah and John the Baptist begin to pour out on the earth to bring restoration to family spiritual and natural.

We will see more signs manifest in the sky, the earth and the sea; a lot of signs will take place to speak to us about the coming of the Lord. Although many nations will want to suppress evangelism, man will have no excuse, because God will use the environment to speak. (Psalm 19: 1 – 7). We learn the things of God general revelation of His creation (Romans 1: 19 – 20), and by specific revelation by His inspired Word. (Psalm 19: 1-7, Hebrews 1: 11, Hebrews 11: 1 – 3). Everything was formed, shaped, and created by His Word.

A Shift

There is going to be a shift taking place within the earth to reap the harvest. Similarly, when Jesus was on earth, there was a shift from the Jews to the Gentiles because His own did not accept Him. God has been speaking to scientists, weathermen, marine biologists, economists, and astrologers about the things that are happening. The signs of time. He is also speaking to them to use them to carry the message that no one will have any excuse not to make it in. (Deuteronomy 17: 3).

There are many people including scientists who are worshiping the heavenly bodies as was done in ancient Egypt in the days of Moses. They worship the ancient Egyptian gods for wealth and money; and they enslave God's people. In the same way that God anointed Moses to set His people free to worship Him in spirit and in truth, we are about to see it happen again. We will see an eclipse to take place to deal with their gods. God will demonstrate His power again to this generation that they will worship Him. He will also demonstrate His power over the sun. The sun is the most potent religious symbol of Egypt. (Exodus 10: 21).

Many for wealth and power worship the sun god and Pharaoh himself Amon-Ra, which is the sun god, and God is going to bring a direct frontal attack on the Pharaoh of this time. The witchcraft will be dealt with. Joshua 10: 12. There are a lot of people who work, and they use the sun and the moon, and they worship them which is part of Baal worship. God wants those who worship the sun gods to repent. Everyone should read Ezekiel 8: 16 – 18 and Ezekiel 9: 2. They fill the land with violence. Joel 2: 30 – 31 also speak of the eclipse and there is an eclipse coming and every man must prepare. The earth is about to plunge into spiritual darkness, which we will see a lot of war and violence, and the birthing of the new world order. There will be redemption for those who turn to the

Lord, but disaster for those who refuse. We will see a universal outpouring of the Spirit, especially among the children. There are many of Pharaoh's magicians. There are many magicians surrounding Pharaoh's leaders which influence them to do evil in the sight of God. God is about to purge them to come around these leaders. God is expecting salvation to all those that are unsaved, and it is time for them to come home. He will use all of those who are willing to give justice to the poor, the fatherless and the widow. (Isaiah 45: 6; 2 Kings 23: 5 – 11; Jeremiah 8: 1 – 2).

The Symbols of Matthew 24: 29 – 30

These are the symbols to watch; always have your eyes on them. (Luke 21: 25 – 28).

✓ The Sun
✓ The Star
✓ The Moon
✓ The Earth

These will be darkness, stars falling, moon not giving light, and the earth shaken. The meaning of these symbols speaks of the returning of Christ, the gathering of God's people. There will be increase of angel for the gathering of the harvest, a blowing of the four winds within the earth. (Mark 13: 24; Revelation 8: 19), we will see distress of nations, war, tsunami, tidal wave, plane falling from the sky. We will see the Babylonian system crashing, but God will seal a few remnants to reap the harvest in the earth. We will see a showdown of false prophets from the true prophets Micah 3: 6. The Glory of God will reveal in the earth.

Signs and Symbols Quick References

Signs and symbols are critical to learn in understanding the Book of Revelation. Look at the following:

The Church in Revelation 17 woman with child symbolize the Church.

The Seal symbolizes confirmation or approval or belonging to God.

The Star speaks of descendants and Jesus Christ.

Horn symbolizes power and things under the anointing.

Angel always speaks of the Church, real angel or it can be a Pastor.

Trumpets symbolize announcements, gathering or judgment.

Head symbolizes leader, authority and power.

Crown symbolizes King, power, authority.

The Sea Of Glass – symbolizes transparency. Revelation 15: 1 – 8. Sea also means people.

Trees symbolize leader good or bad, nations and kingdoms.

Throne symbolizes seat of power or place of authority. Revelation 4: 2 – 3.

Horse Rider symbolizes time, nature of time or work. The front half of the horse means the first part of time or work or beginning. The back half of the horse symbolizes last half of time or work or end.

Quarter Horse symbolizes strong success, and deception. Revelation 6: 2.

White Horse symbolizes international power and politics in the form of military conquest so as deception. Many countries will be conquered by the anti-Christ through loans that they are borrowing, countries. It is also warning for countries that are now borrowing loans from countries which are influenced by the anti-Christ. These countries that keep borrowing, many will default on their loans and will be taken over by the anti-Christ.

The Red Horse symbolizes civil war and strife.

The Black Horse symbolizes economic disruption, inflation, things will become scarce or shortage, labor problems, low wages, rampant starvation. It is critical for God's people to begin to stockpile.

The Pale Horse symbolizes disease and death, devastation, shortage of medication, more problem within the ocean, fish will die.

The Frog symbolizes false prophets, perversion, unclean defiling word.

The Eagle symbolizes the prophetic, leadership.

The Dog symbolizes two-fold meaning: watchman, enemies, ingratitude. If the dog bites you, they are biting the hand that feeds them. It can mean also backsliding.

Vehicle symbolizes family, school or church and the size is very important.

Airport symbolizes a place of transition, prepare to move, evangelism, missionary, equipping and sending.

Leviathan symbolizes alligator Psalm 74 and Job 41. Leviathan is the one that causes the king of pride, causes division in the Church, nation and attack the finances.

School depends to which level of school. Example: high school, primary/elementary and university. It is a place of learning and different dimensions of God. Old School speaks of generation curses or past issues or evil altars.

The Dove: symbols of the Holy Spirit. The Dove symbolizes gentleness, purity, peace, tenderness.

Oil symbolizes beauty, life, usefulness. Water symbolizes the Word, cleansing, soul, and it purifies. Exodus 36: 25 – 27, Exodus 47: 1, Exodus 17: 6.

The Wind symbolizes the regenerative work of the Holy Spirit, and it also symbolizes life-giving and purify operation.

The Seal means confirmation, ownership or approval or belonging to God. Ephesians 1: 13.

Fire symbolizes purging, purification, and illumination. Jeremiah 20: 9, Matthew 3: 11.

What are the Seven Seals

The seven seals catastrophic events that will take place in the end time. It will be the judgment of God upon the earth. It will be like the seven plagues in Exodus. Revelation 6: 1 – 17 and Revelation 8: 1 – 5. The seal will break open and within those seals are prophetic instructions that will be executed in the earth.

- Introduce the anti-Christ. Revelation 6: 2. The White horse rider, the war against the saint, deception.

- Speaks about the Red Horse Rider

- Black Horse Rider which includes death and famine

- The Pale Horse and plague and virus

- The martyred which those with the white robes Revelation 6: 12 – 14

- Earthquakes and disasters will take place; mountains and islands will disappear and there will be significant dislocation.

- There will be a silence in the heaven, as war will be completed.

The Book of Revelation does not necessarily mean that it is in the sequence of how it is being written. We know in part, and we prophesy in part, else we maybe far ahead than where we are. Hence, we must be ready.

The Trumpets

In the Book of Revelation, trumpet is used to build anticipation, announcement or warning is about to take place. It is a time of horrendous judgment on the earth in the Book of Revelation 8: 1 – 2, Revelation 6: 9 – 11, there are seven trumpets mentioned. The first one that will blow:

- Devastation to the earth. Revelation 8: 7

- It will target towards the sea. Revelation 8: 8 – 9

- Water will be affected Revelation 8: 10 – 11

- Attack the sky, the sun will be affected, the moon and the star. Revelation 8: 12. The first four trumpets will focus on the earth, the water, the sea, and the sky. Then the last three trumpets in Revelation, we will see the manifestation of the three woes on the earth. Revelation 8: 13. But in the middle of the judgment, God will part the sea, if man will repent. Many will not repent.

- The fifth trumpet. Revelation 9: 1 – 12, demonic power, locusts, men will be tormented.

- The sixth trumpet Revelation 9: 13 – 21. Death: one third of the globe will die. Revelation 9: 20 – 21 says *"But the rest of mankind, who were mot killed by these plagues, did not repent of the works of their hands, that they should not worship demons, and idols of gold, silver, brass, stone, and wood, which can neither see nor hear nor walk." "And they did not repent of their murders or their sorceries or their sexual immorality or their thefts."*

- Completion. Read Revelation 10 and Revelation 11 to have a better understanding.

Numerical Systems of Identification

Governments in different nations globally are employing or are seeking to employ the use of a numerical systems of identification – a national identification system (NIDS) within their country for the purpose of tracking their citizens, temporary and permanent residents for various reasons. It is also referred to in other nations as a national identification number, national identity number, or national insurance number or JMBG/EMBG, which is a Unique Master Citizen Number that was assigned to every citizen of the former Yugoslav republics of the Socialist

Federal Republic of Yugoslavia. Interestingly, the Unique Master Citizen Number continues to be used in almost all the countries that were created after the dissolution of Yugoslavia.

There are many debates going on about identification systems that will be implemented in the end time. Upon reading Revelation 13, it is clear, that numerical systems of identification would be prevalent in the End Times. It is critical for us to understand that Revelation 13 particularly verses 13 – 16, speaks of the number 666 – the mark of the beast). However, 666 is more than a number, it's all about the definition of that number. It is about who will pledge allegiance to in the end time.

The number 6 represents *image, idol, form, labor,* and is also the number representing *man, sin, flesh,* and *carnality.* It also signifies *falling short of God's perfection.*

So, what the anti-Christ will do in the end time, is have one global data information system giving them access on all individuals globally by just pressing a button. The anti-Christ will come through the economic and the security systems; and international travel will also be affected. One passport will become obsolete, and a new passport system created. It will be difficult for one to transact business meaning buying and selling, unless they abide by that system.

Furthermore, the Enemy, through the anti-Christ wants to re-create man in *his* image in order to have his own army of followers. He seeks to copy the original and "re-wire" mankind for his own evil purposes and as a challenge to the plan of God, because God said, *"Let us make man in our own image."* (Genesis 1: 26)

What this really means is that your information will be absent anywhere around the world, whether through market information, insurance, banking and will tie to government benefits. Your health information, which is supposed to be private, will be government information. Watch the health passport that they are proposing. Very shortly, all your information will be on your debit or credit card, whether you are vaccinated or not vaccinated. Government will operate like a god.

The anti-Christ will want to be the supreme being, so they will ensure that a system is in place so that regardless of the government department you go to transact business, every other government department will be able to access your information. As a result, there will be no privacy. In the same way that it happened in Japan, where government departments can access information among each other about their citizens.

The anti-Christ also wants to establish a counterfeit trading. As such, a National Identification System will be used to take away the assets, there will be no protection of your information. Every system which does not give one the options of choosing, is the anti-Christ system. You must always have your right to sign up online whether online banking or transacting business inside of the banking center. There must be a choice, and no one should be forced to get involve into something that they do not feel secure to do so.

While the world has gone online with everything, including commerce, finance, and socializing, and has become comfortable settling in the online zone, enjoying the ease of the digital world, many of them are being hacked. What it means is that just as easily, one can be rich today and broke tomorrow. We should never ever forget about the hacking information that was exposed on social network regarding Facebook.

Not People, Numbers

What that should tell us is that we will no longer be recognized as human beings but instead as numbers. So, the question is "What will happen when man begin to hack the national identification system, and utilize the information for their own benefit? You can be bandaged from society, government can say you no longer exist, if they want to come against you. This is an identity crisis. Your assets of land and property will be in danger. You will be tracked everywhere you go, and there will be no privacy. Christians will begin to get blocked from having certain services because of our moral and standards. It will be similar with the Nazis and the tattoos. Even robots will have our information.

As we read the Book of Revelation, many may think that the mark may be in the hand, but it is not necessarily so. (Revelation 14: 9 – 10). The scripture speaks oaths of allegiance – your right hand represents power and honor and speaks also of agreement.

The left hand speaks of something spiritually, so it will be critical who we honor or what we agree to in the end time. Our forehead symbolizes that which is prominent and determine the identity of something or someone. (Jeremiah 3: 3, Revelation 22: 4). All these IDs carry RFID Chip in them. So, the mark does not necessarily be that it will be in the hand, it can come in different areas. The anti-Christ system is a system built without God. Building nations without God is still the spirit of Nimrod in manifestation. (Genesis 11: 1 - 9).

So, we will see different identification systems come in place, but they will all merge into one major system. Most IDs want scan, face, eyes, fingerprint, and retinal scan. These days there are different apps on our cellular phones to track individuals and the COVID-19 App to find our location.

The enemy always builds ahead and wait for an opportunity to roll out certain features and certain laws. Man will be like bar code data that relates to the object which is attached to identify a product and to scan a product. It is said that bar codes made up of 13 vertical lines. The number 13 represents rebellion, rejection, and revolution. (Genesis 14: 4). It is also said that there are 13 evils. (Mark 7: 21 – 22).

The barcodes we see on products identify and track sales, and if they can do so with products, then they can find a way to do it with people as well. It therefore means that man may be entering into a new level of bondage and slavery. So, things will be about control, allegiance, power, worship, manipulation, deception, bondage, movement, economics, faith, wealth, and these are going to be very significant words in our vocabulary in these End Times.

We need to understand that at the root of it all is the fact that Satan cannot be in all places one time, and so, in order to have the kind of control he wants, he is attempting to mirror the omnipresence of God by imposing these systems. Those who accept the mark, the beast will be owned by government. However, as the enemy gathers his followers, God is sealing His people. Ultimately, it is all about allegiance. The decisions we make in the end time are critical because they depend on and determine who owns you. Satan will promise prosperity and wealth in exchange for being a part of his system in the end time, and he can use something as simple as paying people to be guinea pigs to take a vaccine sends a message.

The enemy wants to control what the Babylonian system refers to as the Gate of God. The name Babel in Genesis 11: 9 means "confusion" in the Hebrew word; however, in Babylonian, the Tower of Babel was called *Bab-ilu*, meaning "Gate of God"; which sounded like the Hebrew word *Babel*, or *Bavel* in pronunciation and led to the play on words in the scripture – Confusion (*Hebrew meaning*) vs. the Gate of God (*Babylonian*). The Tower of Babel was a portal the enemy wanted to control but God thwarted his plans.

What The Anti-Christ System Will Bring

The globe will plunge into confusion as the anti-Christ advances. Genesis 10, Joel 3: 2, Zachariah 14: 2. These Identification Cards will be the end of privacy and will fuel increase in crime at every level. Furthermore:

More hit men will come out of the woodworks.

- Rapists and Sexual Predators will have access to personal information and will know everything about their potential victims. The information gleaned from these identification cards will also be used to track your movements and activities, tracking you as you visit other countries.

- Tax Collectors will have an unprecedented level of access to your information. They will use it to be more exact in taxes and keep abreast of payments. They will use it to block you from travelling, especially if you owe tax.

- It will also be a problem with health issues, contamination of one's blood, tampering of with one's blood work and wrong diagnostics, missing medical files and deletion of medical files, wrong surgery will take place,

Additionally, because the corruption levels will increase in the End Times, missing police reports, bribery and exploitation of the traffic citation system will also increase. There will be unsolicited surveillance of private citizens, whether or not they are involved in criminal activities, because the anti-Christ wants to be worshipped, and they want to manipulate and control. Many laws will change, and many Christians will become enemies of the state. Laws will be passed so that the hate crime bill can be used against us.

All these systems/laws are being put in place to make war against the saints of God. (Revelation 12: 17). We must understand that the anti-Christ system is about creating a secular, Godless system, and must exclude any religious systems.

The anti-Christ will remove anything God established, The Church, The Family, Marriage, and the Original Genders. He will work overtime to try to remove or taint everything God did. Poorer countries will seek the anti-Christ for solution and form allegiance with them. So, it will be critical what documents nations sign overtime, as most nations will get into covenant and treaties in order to survive which will bring the people into captivity.

What Does "The Mark" Mean

When we speak of the mark of the beast, we must determine what the term "mark" means. A mark can mean an engraving, an imprint, branded, documented, and stamped. The key word is allegiance. During the pandemic there were many that were forced to take the vaccine, while they say it is not mandatory for you to take it, they still go about setting up laws to block you, but within the schools, once you are not vaccinated, you no longer have a job. But this is deception. It is critical in the end time for Christians to be independent, owning their own home and their own business.

Chapter 12

END-TIME STRATEGY OF THE ANTI-CHRIST AND THE ANTI-CHRIST SYSTEMS

The books of Daniel and Revelation reveal to us the deep insights of the tactics and strategies of the Anti-Christ – the anti-Christian governments, systems and political power, as well as the philosophies, ideologies, and deceptive, seductive anti-Christian society, commerce and culture the world is seeking to create. They are attempting to have a world without God and the things of God.

The Key Sectors

We will see continued reformation in the Banking Sector, National Security, The Pharmaceutical and Medical Industries and the Media. The Media will act as the Public Relations arm for the anti-Christ in the end-time, so the hands of the journalists will be tied. They will simply collect money to publicize the philosophies expressed and indoctrinate the masses because of its influence among the masses. So, while we will see global economic decline, we will see many media houses merge, while others close and some will take the bait. So, it will not be fair journalism. The anti-Christ will dictate who heads certain sectors, so that they can dictate the level of influence Christians have (if any) in any sector.

Division Of The Masses

Another aspect of their strategy is to divide and distract the masses through gender issues, racial issues, cultural matters as well as the issue of moral versus immoral. They will create problems just so they can introduce the solutions they want in order to maintain control of the society. So that, the more problems that exist – whether it be security-related or cyber issues – they will use it to bring in anti-Christ systems such as Radio Frequency Identification (RFIDs), DNA collection for tracking and those who will suffer the most are those below the poverty line. They will give to those people, but it will come at a high price. They will have to agree to certain systems that would violate everything they believe in, especially their beliefs.

Sovereignty At Stake

We are seeing these days, significant numbers of rulings on sexual rights over and above religious rights and freedoms. The anti-Christ will be such a force, that the judicial systems that now exist will only be able to fall in line. Judges will not be promoted until they yield to the system that will be in existence. Many nations will be at the mercy of other nations, and promised economic growth, further development, grants, contracts and loans, but within the fine print, they will have to agree to those nations' terms and the sovereignty of the receiving nations will be at stake.

It is very important for the electorate to know what the fine print says regarding the expectation of each nation;

as well as the timeline for implementation. It is not about which political party is better able to run a country, but which is better able/suited to carry out the system of the anti-Christ and that will determine what happens in the next five (5) years.

The Church and the Symbols

It is critical for the Church to learn about numbers, symbols and what the new norms will be. Most Pastors are looking for the number 666, but we need to know what the number six (6) represents. It represents, carnality, sin, flesh, man, labor and information will be key. We must remember that "Babylon" is a system without God, and scrutiny of all political persons coming into the system is key. It will become even more important to know their beliefs, mandates and motives. The churches will need to combine their resources in order to deal with the beast and Pastors need to understand that they are no fried to the system. Daniel 11: 37 is clear – "He shall regard neither the God of his fathers nor the desire of women, nor regard any god; for he shall exalt himself above them all."

Take note that the woman symbolizes the Church, so he will not tolerate Christianity, especially in the marketplace. It will be difficult for churches who receive government grants and any form of support Globally. Those churches will be in line with the requirements of the system. So, they won't be able to speak against population control, abortion, and other matters pertinent to the freedoms of the Church.

Journalists who genuinely want certain truths to come out will be muzzled or killed so they will need to start their own business.

Jesus Christ Vs. The Anti-Christ

First, in order to understand the anti-Christ in this end time, we should ensure we don't confuse the Anti-Christ – which is the Man of Sin in the scriptures, with the anti-Christ system, which is the system set up to execute the instructions of the Anti-Christ (the man), in the various sectors, such as Politics, the Church and Business.

The term "anti" means "against, instead of, or, in the place of", and in this case, the word Anti-Christ means in place of Jesus Christ.

Judge The Anti-Christ Systems

The Anti-Christ and anti-Christ systems being pushed are in complete rebellion against the Almighty God, and he will use many to bring reformation and legislate his Babylonian system in the end time. Any system that is going to be against the word of God is the anti-Christ system.

1 John 2: 18 says "Little children, it is the last hour; and as you have heard that the Antichrist is coming, even now many antichrists have come, by which we know that it is the last hour."

We must always use the Bible to judge any system implemented by government to see whether or not it is in agreement with Christ or if it is anti-Christ.

The question we need to ask is this; "Is your government functioning under Divine Authority or are they functioning as the divine authority? We also need to know this; "to whom are they pledging allegiance? Are they promoting sin or righteousness? Is the nation promoting a Christian or Secular society? Are they promoting freedom of worship and freedom of speech?

Built On Deception

The anti-Christ system rules with lies and deception. They also create problems within the society in order to bring their own anti-Christ solutions. Understand that the mark of the beast is all about allegiance, and there is no middle ground. The system of the anti-Christ is there to destroy your faith in God and pull you away from the faith so that your name will not be written in the Lamb's Book of Life.

The anti-Christ system is about money, fame, power, artificial kingdoms and economies set up to deceive the masses. With something as simple as a virus, they will set up vaccines and promote it as the alternative – the savior! Many will come and portray themselves to be the true ones who are of God, and even present products as the only alternative – when Jesus is the Only Way. We must remember that there is no one who can supersede Jesus! (Colossians 2: 16).

152

PR For The Anti-Christ

We are now seeing media becoming the PR Team for the Anti-Christ and the systems. It seems investigative Journalism is a thing of the past. They are simple drunk with the wine of the Anti-Christ.

If someone says that the vaccine is the only way to get back to a "normal life", that would be in conflict with the Word of God and with Jesus. Isn't He *Jehovah Rophe* – The Lord My Healer?

The system of the anti-Christ will want to discredit God's true servants and try to shut down the truth, while labelling every Christian as an uneducated fundamentalist, and/or a fanatic. Their goal is to divide, discredit, deceive and to destroy; that is why, as Christians, we must discern the dragon in this end time. The dragon cannot be discerned by way of education and logic, but by Divine Revelation and the Word of God. The plan of the anti-Christ is to set up an earthly government – a counterfeit of the Trinity, as well as images for people to worship. (Revelation 13: 15; Revelation 19: 20). When the scripture speaks of "giving life", it could be referring to Artificial Intelligence and Tracking Systems, and the Digital/Virtual platforms facilitate it all. However, despite their efforts, all the implementations of the anti-Christ will fail.

Antics Of The Anti-Christ

Remember, the Anti-Christ will create events in the end time and use them as opportunities to implement their system. For example, COVID-19 has opened the door for many things to be introduced – Apps, surveillance devices, biometrics and other such things under the disguise of health, safety, security and economic development.

The Anti-Christ is after one world order, one world currency and a borderless society. He wants to be like God. He wants to build a system where he can have control of all information for everyone everywhere at the tip of his fingers. The signing of the Peace Treaty with the USA, Israel and the Arab nations is the fulfillment of Ezekiel 38 and 38.

- ✓ The body parts, animals and other images are critical to understanding end time revelations. For example, the forehead symbolizes identification purposes (NIDS, Biometrics and others) – that which is prominent; something or someone. (Revelation 13: 16 – 18, Revelation 22: 4; Jeremiah 3: 3)

- ✓ Realize that the right hand means oath of allegiance which signifies power, honor and natural strength. It is interesting that in order to test for the COVID-19 when you are entering a building, they scan your head and your right hand. Could it be a major dress rehearsal for the system that is already being put in place which will not allow you to buy or sell without a "mark"?

✓ The number "6" means "flesh, carnal, man, evil, Satan". The current computer code is 6 and it will extend to other 6's. Governments will want to operate as if they are gods and will attach your blood type, tax information and all your assets once you go into a building then they will have access to all your information.

✓ You have heard of things being stored in the "cloud", but who owns and monitors this cloud? We know that the devil operates in the second heaven, which is where we see the physical clouds, sky and so on. So who is controlling the information stored in "the cloud"?

There are 6 different kinds of COVID-19 in existence. They say 6 people are safer together in the pandemic. Then they say stay 6 feet apart to maintain proper social distancing. Much of how the world is run seems to hinge on 6's. Six also is the number that represents SIN.

It is critical for us also to read Daniel 7 to unlock the code. Many global leaders will be taking allegiance with the Anti-Christ rather than with Christ in order to maintain political power. It will first start with the poorer ones in the society. They will need to depend on the state for survival, but it will come with their allegiance, particularly through voting, which is easier to manipulate.

Social Media and Networks

Matthew 24: 14 says, "And this gospel of the kingdom will be preached in all the world as a witness to all the nations, and then the end will come."

The pandemic has accelerated this prophecy. Zoom and other such platform have connected and continue to connect people globally, which is causing that Word to be fulfilled. Evangelists no longer have to physically enter a country in order to spread the gospel. The introduction of Artificial Intelligence (AI) has created a borderless global society in which to do business. It will be interesting to see what will happen with the Airline Industry.

The global pandemic has caused millions of churches to be closed – some by persecution, some by way of fear. In the West, many Pastors are being jailed as they defend their religious rights, while politicians are proudly glorifying the things of darkness. Aren't these signs of the end-time?

We are now seeing a new level of deception hitting earth. Some are offering "opportunities" to enter the lottery by taking the "jab"/(vaccine). Some are being offered the equivalent of less than a night's dinner to take the vaccine while the poor the fatherless and the widow are dying of hunger and neglect, and furthermore, no other sickness really matters.

We are now seeing some of the greatest deceptions in the pharmaceutical industry. (Revelation 18)

Recognize that Revelation 18: 23 says "The light of a lamp shall not shine in you anymore, and the voice of bridegroom and bride shall not be heard in you anymore. For your merchants were the great men of the earth, for by your sorcery all the nations were deceived." This scripture was in reference to Babylon, and the word "sorceries" here is translated from the Greek work "pharmakeia" from which we get the word English word "pharmacy." So, this industry today fights against God-given, natural, simple remedies and are making enormous sums of money doing so.

Revelation 13: 16 – 17 reminds us, "He causes all, both small and great, rich and poor, free and slave, to receive a mark on their right hand or on their foreheads, and that no one may buy or sell except one who has the mark or the name of the beast, or the number of his name."

It is practically historic that today, nurses in Christian hospitals, policemen, soldiers and other essential personnel are being denied certain salient services and are in fact being forced out of their jobs because it is now mandatory (although silently stated) that they take a vaccine. Banks are also included in this web of deception. Aren't these the signs of times?

Mainstream Media

We are now seeing the global power of mainstream media censoring and banning anyone who does not agree with nor share their points of view. Algorithms have been set to pick up on certain key words and phrases they have determined, in order to censor and block certain persons and groups they don't like.

Politicians are being reverted from key decision-makers and influencers to marketing and sales reps for their new "boss".

Aren't these the signs of times?

Stand Firm

Every Christian must stand firm in their faith, hold on to their beliefs and discern, the times, seasons, actions and activities taking place today and maintain their position in the Kingdom of God. Ensure that regardless of what they do, your soul is secure in God.

Chapter 13

END TIME SIGNS, TIMES AND SEASONS

Impending Judgement and Trouble

It is critical for us to understand Times and Seasons. We are in a season where mighty thunders will roar. Prophetically, thunder symbolizes signs of times, change without understanding as well as dispensational changes – even regarding how God deals with His people.

When the Father speaks, He thunders! (John 12: 28 – 29). The Father is about to speak. Psalms 18: 13 - 14 also reveals that there are times when thunder roars that there are "...Hailstones and coals of fire." When the thunder roars look out for lightning also. His arrow will also be released to scatter the enemies. We will also see a shaking of the earth spiritually and naturally. Shifting will take place in other sectors.

He will also pour out His glory in the earth; signs will be in the skies and in the clouds. He will be dealing with the foundations of the hills. God will shake the high places. All the places that have exalted themselves will be shaken. The righteous should not be afraid, but they should get ready. God will exalt them and lift them up. He will fast forward blessing. The roar will also affect the economic systems in the earth and many will crash.
Even the weatherman will tell you, "When thunder roars, stay indoors!" Always keep in mind that if you can hear thunder, you are close enough to be struck by lightning.

.

Seek shelter immediately. According to Psalm 91, God is our shelter, so ensure that you are in the Shelter when the Thunder Roars!

Trumpet

The trumpet symbolizes the announcement and warning and the calling of the assembly to wake up. It is the time to worship Him in Spirit and in truth. The voice of the prophets and the Fivefold proclaiming the good news, also admonishing us to be ready for the rapture.

Get ready Church – it is not business as usual. *Be Ready! A New Season And A New Day Has Begun!*

End-Times And Signs Everywhere

Matthew 24: 3 and 7 says "Now as He sat on the Mount of Olives, the disciples came to Him privately, saying, "Tell us, when will these things be? And what will be the sign of Your coming, and of the end of the age? ... nation will rise against nation, and kingdom against kingdom. And there will be famines, pestilences, and earthquakes in various places."

We are seeing the manifestation of these words right before our eyes. There are signs everywhere and rapid manifestations. We are seeing the falling away of saints, which is apostasy, happening in every direction. We also see the church embracing a "death culture" and satanic doctrines. We see signs in the weather pattern including

160

record-level, earthquakes, famines, pestilences and increasing global deception, particularly in the area of health and sciences. There is great lack of trust in God which has led to millions falling into scientific deception. Most say they have taken the vaccine for a better future (or so they think). We have seen the LGBTQ+ expand and many churches and nations have facilitated and bowed to their bidding for monetary gain. Churches are partnering with evil organizations, and the spirit of mammon have taken over nation leaders and some within the body of Christ. Many Christians have turned their backs on God for money. Many prophets have become religious in their thinking. Our weather patterns throughout the globe has changed drastically. Aren't these signs everywhere?

End Time Signs And Symbols

End Time signs and symbols are visible everywhere in our world today. Throughout the entire globe we are seeing activities that speak to that. Furthermore, we are now seeing a dress rehearsal of sorts of Revelation 13.

In order for the saints to not be deceived, it is critical to understand signs and symbols in the end time. For example

The **White horse** is a symbol of international power and politics. In the form of military conquest and global deception. Many countries will be conquered through loans that they are borrowing from other countries. Warning for countries that keep borrowing loans. Many loans will be default and many countries will find themselves in trouble.

The **Red Horse** is a symbol of civil war and strife.

The **Black Horse** is symbol of economic disruption. Inflation, things will become scarce or shortage. There will be labor problems – low wages; rampant starvation, and God wants us to stockpile water and gold. It also means there will be great shifts in the global economy!

The **Pale Horse** is a symbol of disease and death, devastation that will break out. It means that there will be a shortage of medication that will take place. So, more problems within the ocean as more fish will die. (Study Revelation, read the seven letters to the church.)

Discern

God's people need to discern in the end time. They should in no way listen to the excuse that things are implemented to better govern the people. The book of Genesis did not state that man was given the authority to have dominion over man or for man to be worshiped. Worship belongs only to God. The Anti-Christ is looking for worship and for people to bow down.
The kneeling of members of the Black Lives Matter group, and others in the sports industry are all dress rehearsals of what is to come. Unless mankind looks to God, many will bow, but it will be too late.

The Almond Tree And The Boiling Pot

Understanding symbols in the end-time are critical.

The Boiling Pot represents God's judgement, calamity and terror, from the north, since during that time most of the invaders of Israel and Judah came from that direction.

The steam of this boiling pot represented God's judgments, which are often compared to a fire, as the afflictions of Israel were to a smoking furnace. (Jeremiah 1: 13; Genesis 15:17.)

The Boiling Pot also symbolizes doctrine, traditions, determination through a person. The pot further denoted the empire of the Chaldeans, lying to the north of Judea, and pouring forth its multitudes like a thick vapor.

Jeremiah 1: 11 – 13 tells us:

"Moreover the word of the Lord came to me, saying, "Jeremiah, what do you see?" And I said, "I see a branch of an almond tree." Then the Lord said to me, "You have seen well, for I am ready to perform My word." And the word of the Lord came to me the second time, saying, "What do you see?" And I said, "I see a boiling pot, and it is facing away from the north."

In this Scripture, we see where God tested the prophetic understanding and growth of His prophets, to see whether or not they understood the times and seasons.

Generally speaking, the almond tree blooms early in the spring. It is the first tree to bloom in the winter; and when it blossoms, it is symbolic of spring in the air. In the Hebrew culture, the almond tree and the action of Jeremiah watching (as a watchman would) symbolizes new season, hope, joy and resurrection. It meant things would begin to spring forth again. To some extent it meant replenishing and restoration. The prophet of God must know what season they are in so that they could accurately guide the nation. It also represents God swiftly fulfilling His promise of upcoming exile and destruction. The almond tree blossoms as early in the season. This showed imminent calamity for the wicked*-

.

Are the nations ready to deal with the judgement calamity and terror that is about to come upon the globe? It is critical therefore, for the peoples of the nations to stock up on the following:

Masks	Sanitizers	Toothpaste
Bleach	Wipes	Pampers
Pull-ups	Baby Formula	Bath Soap
Lamps	Candles	Matches
Olive Oil	Garlic	Tents
Water	Basins/Tubs	Medical Supplies

.

Vitamins   Canned Goods Feminine Products

Batteries   Matches/Lighters

Bitter And Sweet

Almond comes in 2 species – bitter and sweet. So, we will see the manifestation of 2 events – bitter and sweet. Ultimately, we will see redemption and destruction.

Jeremiah 31: 27 – 28 reminds us, *"Behold, the days are coming, says the Lord, that I will sow the house of Israel and the house of Judah with the seed of man and the seed of beast. And it shall come to pass, that as I have watched over them to pluck up, to break down, to throw down, to destroy, and to afflict, so I will watch over them to build and to plant, says the Lord."*

While God's faithful will walk in prosperity, the enemies of God will experience the judgement of God.

While God watches over His people, He will build up and plant them. However, the enemy will be uprooted and broken down. Breakdown is a must in order to build. We will see this happen globally.

The Hebrew meaning for the word *"almond"* is *"sha-kade"* and the root of the word *"almond," "sha-ked,"* is identical to the verb *"sha-kad,"* which means *"to be diligent," "to strive," "steadfast."* These are the qualities that any good watchman must possess.

God has a time to perform every prophetic word – whether positive or negative. We are in a time where God is ready to perform His word, hence, the watchman must watch, hasten, anticipate, be sleepless, alert, vigilant and on the look-out.

Spring Begins

In the Northern Hemisphere this year, Spring begins on March 20, 2022 and ends on June 21, 2022. So, in the first 19 days of March, we need to be on the watch. It is important to note that while Spring happens in the Northern Hemisphere – in countries such as Canada, the USA, the Caribbean Islands and the West Indies, it is Winter in the Southern Hemisphere – in countries such as Australia, New Zealand, Antarctica, major parts of South America, about one-third of Africa, and some islands of mainland Asia.

Jeremiah 1: 13 – 15 speaks of the calamity and terror that will come out of the North. The Babylonians are the major instruments used by God to punish His enemies. Interestingly, the Northernmost nations of the world include Greenland/Denmark, Canada, Russia, Norway, United States, Finland, Sweden, and Iceland. Today, most if not all of these nations are hotbeds of activity.

Knowing The Times And Seasons

There are some people throughout the globe who have a God-given gift to understand times and seasons. However, this understanding is not limited or exclusive to such ones. We all have the capacity to understand times and seasons, and it is critical for us to do so. (1 Chronicles 12: 32)

Since the beginning of the year many have returned to their old habits. Many are trying to re-capture 3 years past and continue to hope to return to normal. They want to go back to business as usual without making any adjustments or changes. This is particularly so in the music and entertainment industry and among politicians, businessmen and even the Church, where so many of them are proclaiming some things upon themselves about being the G.O.A.T. - The Greatest Of All Time. Some call themselves "undisputed champion", others say they are the greatest political strategist. People must all remember that 2022 is a Shemita year - a year of the Lord's release. It would also do them well to remember that this is a year of light, truth and the year of the Son Who is Jesus, hence, the unexpected will take place. It is a time of repentance and reflection. Someone will have a billion on Monday and zero on Tuesday.

Climate Change

Climate Change will continue to be of the utmost importance. We are now having highly unusual weather patterns. Freezing weather in tropical areas. We must remember that God created the earth to work in a natural specific order; what if tampering of the climate/weather patterns has taken place? It is not impossible. Tampering with the natural order of creation is nothing new, and such action is geared toward causing disorder in the natural flow of things, as in Genesis 1, and this is exactly what he enemy wants to happen.

Hence there has to be a reset and it is necessary. It will not only be from an economic standpoint but in all areas including the weather. So, after the reset, when the original falls back into place once more, some of those happenings will begin to look highly unusual. We will see the wind of the Spirit begin to deal with the contrary wind; and remember, the weather always tells us what is going on in the realm of the Spirit. It is the wind of the Holy Spirit that deals with

The wind and moisture levels always determine how cold the weather feels.

Wormwood

Wormwood is recorded in the Book of Revelation 8: 10 – 11, which says, *"Then the third angel sounded: And a great star fell from heaven, burning like a torch, and it fell on a third of the rivers and on the springs of water. The name of the star is Wormwood. A third of the waters became wormwood, and many men died from the water, because it was made bitter."*
Many scholars say it has to do with meteorites falling to hit the earth and contaminate the water. Others say it

168

may be nuclear weapons or the bitter events that will be taking place. Interestingly, the Greek word for Wormwood is *"apsinthos"* which is a poisonous plant used for various digestive and intestinal issues – including bladder disease, intestinal spasms and other related issues. There are several other scriptures that mention "wormwood. See also Deuteronomy 29: 18, Proverbs 5:4, Amos 5: 7, Jeremiah 9: 15, Jeremiah 23: 15; Lamentations 3: 19. Furthermore, Wormwood cleanses, boosts the immune system, and nourishes the intestines. It is also very good for energy management. Wormwood is diverse, so, it is therefore critical for us to watch that word "Wormwood" to see if it refers to negative or positive happenings.

Money Changers

There are many who are utilizing the Church for various personal reasons. God specifically outlined the purpose of His house. He said, "My house is a house of prayer. (Matthew 21: 12, Mark 11: 15; Luke 19: 45 – 48; John 2: 13 – 16). This eludes to the fact that God is going to start cleansing the Temple. Utilizing the temple for political meetings, fraternal gatherings, Cambio services, gambling and vaccine centers as well as for selling the gifts, and oils, marketing for personal profit, black market activities, thus turning the House of the Lord into a marketplace is unacceptable.

The Lord's Temple should never be allowed to become a trading center and common marketplace, it is to be a House of Prayer . If the leaders and the people who have settled into making the House of the Lord a mere marketplace don't repent, God is going to whip them all out.

Chapter 14

UNDERSTANDING THE WIND AND THE STORM

The word *"wind"* means *"the spirit and the breath."* In the Hebrew word for wind is *'ruah'* which means "breath and spirit." In the Greek it is *"pneuma"* which according to the Oxford Dictionary means the vital spirit and soul creative source. Christ illustrates the working of the Holy Spirit in the regenerating spirit (John 3:8). God used the wind as an instrument to carry out His pleasure and His judgment (Exodus 14: 21, Psalm 78: 26, Psalm 148: 8, 2 Kings 2: 11, Psalm 48: 7 and John 1: 4). Men may use the wind as advantage example farming, energy, sailing (Psalm 1: 4. Psalm 35: 5, Isaiah 17: 13, Acts 27: 40). Each time the Lord is going do something new within nations, He use the wind, whether it bring new order, new change or uproot according to Jeremiah 1:10 – 11. In this scripture we see where Jeremiah used the spirit of prophecy in activating the wind.

Furthermore, Ezekiel 37 speaks of the valley of dry bones where God asked the prophet to prophesy and not preach nor sing. It is here that we see the power of prophecy which brings spiritual regeneration and birth restoration and resurrection which will bring hope to the hopeless, those in exile, curses, miracles. We need the spirit of prophecy to bring a global revival. Prophecy activates the wind and will bring life. It is critical for us as servants of God to know when to begin to prophesy to change a hopeless society where crime and violence and poverty are the order of the day. Many talking about climate change but the only solution to bring true change is prophesying of God's word. The wind is what creates a future, so it is very imperative for us as servants of God to begin to prophesy. Nothing will change or take place without the Holy Spirit and anything the Holy Spirit touches brings life and prosperity. Including:

- ✓ Governance,
- ✓ A righteous nation
- ✓ A move of the spirit
- ✓ For salvation peace prosperity we need the wind.

Any church which refuses to allow the Holy Spirit to manifest in their midst, will be a cemetery, or a graveyard. One of the roles of the prophet's ministry is to speak to dead things to become life. If you read Ezekiel 37, you will have a better understanding of the regenerating power of God.

After the declaration of the prophet there was a sound or noise which symbolizes a move of God. There are many people within the church that are dead spiritually - they have no life in them, no Holy Spirit. Only the Holy Spirit can bring that army that we need in the end time for reaping the harvest to possess our promise land and claim our inheritance. The Bible speaks of four Winds. These are:

- ✓ East Wind
- ✓ South Wind
- ✓ North wind
- ✓ West Wind

The East Wind

God used the East Wind to destroy Pharaoh and his army. In this age, He is still using the east wind to shake oppressors and dictators. From the East Wind comes locust which destroys farming and brings death and destruction (Exodus 10:13), and scorching, which is famine and recession. It also brings massive heat wave on nations causing death to farm products, human beings and we have seen temperature going beyond the normal degrees Fahrenheit (Jonah 4: 8, Genesis 41: 8, 23) and the death of animals. Very shortly we are about to see the death of many animals which will bring chaos upon the globe. God also use the East Wind to dry up sea. (Exodus 14:21). We are about to see global water crisis. We have also seen the East Wind manifested in Job15:2. The east wind is also used to scatter, disrupt, and destroy and expel. (Isaiah 27: 8, Jeremiah 18:7). The East Wind also brings a shout. It is critical for man to be in constant repentance and stop rebel against God or try to use science and logics to fix climate change based off what is happening globally when the solution is repentance.

The South Wind

The South Wind brings peace comfort and stability and protection. We have seen God directed the south wind in Psalm 78:26 and also Job 37:17, Acts 27:13, Acts 28:13. Now more than ever, the need to intercede that the south wind may pour out on nations that we will have prosperity.

The North Wind

The North Wind is found in Proverbs 25: 23 and Songs of Solomon 4: 16 which brings goodness, fruitfulness, blessing, refreshing and growth

The West Wind

The West Wind brings restoration, cleansing deliverance and removal of plagues (Exodus 10: 19). So, based on scriptures, no one can function without the Holy Spirit. He is the one in charge. The Holy Spirit is the one that operates nations and brings solution. Nations ignore the Holy Spirit by rejecting Him for unclean spirits which are bringing the nations into bondage. Many political administrations instead of seeking the Holy Spirit for solution, they have turned to unclean spirits which influence them to pass laws which are anti-Christ and against God's word which further brings the nations into poverty and destruction.

Lessons From The Wind

Apostle Paul, in Acts 27: 14, show us that even during a storm, the Holy Spirit was giving directions to prevent a shipwreck. They ignored His advice and the result ended in a shipwreck. Many political administrations will end up in a shipwreck unless they listen. Most Politicians believe that hiring experts, professionals and even doctors to advise them is the best solution but they are only bringing more problems to the nations.

We have seen firsthand, the damage which the pandemic has brought to the economies of nations globally; but we as believers must put our trust in God and listen to the voice of God, regardless of the storms or contrary winds we face. God's people will be safe.

It was surprising, and unfortunate, that during the pandemic, most churches were closed for no reason, while supermarkets and gambling dens remained open to the public. The voice of God was censored to silence, and it was particularly noticeable on the usually active social media. The churches were censored and blocked and that is why there was initially so much death within the pandemic. Any nation that refuses to listen to the voice of the Lord will face great suffering head on.

God Speaks In The Storm

In the end times we will see many storms and hurricanes. There are also storms of life in many ways, whether it is finance, sickness or other situations. Most times we may encounter storms when we are moving to another phase or to the next level. It is critical for us to discern whether it is God or the enemy, just as Jesus did in Mark 4: 35 - 41 says,

"On the same day, when evening had come, He said to them, "Let us cross over to the other side." Now when they had left the multitude, they took Him along in the boat as He was. And other little boats were also with Him. And a great windstorm arose, and the waves beat into the boat, so that it was already filling. But He was in the

175

stern, asleep on a pillow. And they awoke Him and said to Him, "Teacher, do You not care that we are perishing?" Then He arose and rebuked the wind, and said to the sea, "Peace, be still!" And the wind ceased and there was a great calm. But He said to them, "Why are you so fearful? How is it that you have no faith?" And they feared exceedingly, and said to one another, "Who can this be, that even the wind and the sea obey Him?"

This is great a teaching lesson for us believers, because Jesus shows us that not every storm is of God; and that we have the authority to speak to the storms coming against us. Jesus demonstrates that we have control over the environment. We also have that authority. There are contrary winds which come to stop us or take us down, but we must use those storms to increase our faith (Matthew 8: 23 - 27).

Without a doubt, Jesus reigns over the entire globe, including the elements – the destructive forces, and the evil one. We should never allow contrary winds to stop us from following Jesus. We have the capacity for faith that can make us walk on water. Jesus wants us to have faith.

There are times we must pull away and seek God alone. He wants us on the mountain to lift us higher than the contrary wind. We also see that many times when the spirit moves, we tend to want to call it a ghost and that is we are not properly aligned. Regardless of what happens, when Jesus comes into the vessel every storm ceases. As we go higher in the things of God, He will give us new tactics and strategies to evangelize and to carry out our ministry. We must understand that when God carries His people through a storm, they come out with greater power, greater anointing and greater authority. When the disciples crossed over the contrary wind, they birth a great healing ministry. I believe that there will be a great end time healing ministry that will come through the remnant. We will also see the taking over of the marketplace by God's people. The marketplace will become the next hospital and will embrace God again. We also need to be like the eagle by utilizing the storm to go higher because the eagle use storm to fly higher (Matthew 14: 22-23)

God's Mystery

For us to find out certain mystery from God, we as Christians must follow a certain protocols or path. We must allow the Holy Spirit to reveal to us the answer we seek. The Holy Spirit is the only one that qualifies to reveal the mysteries of God to us. If we do not believe in the Holy Spirit we have already failed. Surprisingly, scientist always wants to reveal certain things to us void of the Holy Spirit. This will cause great harm and death in the end time. They need to stop utilizing people as guinea pigs to see whether or not their experiment works.

It is critical for a man to surrender their life to the Lord (John 3:16) so that He will open their eyes to be more effective in their experiment. If one is not saved or born again, then the information they are giving out is not accurate and these are the person that always want to question the existence of God while embracing both new age philosophy and doctrine of the devil.

There is no way an unsaved person can seek God without first accepting Him. We cannot use our natural way and intellect to understand the mystery of God without the Holy Spirit. Our mind is limited to His understanding without the Holy Spirit. God is a Spirit and He must be worshipped in spirit and truth. Spiritual things have to be spiritually discerned. The flesh cannot deal with spiritual things (2 Corinthians 2:14-15).

The Bible speaks of the natural, the carnal and the spiritual. Only the spiritual man will understand God's word and His ways. You may possess a PhD but the things of God will become foolish because you cannot understand the things of the spirit. Only the Holy Spirit can reveal anything about God and to receive the holy spirit one has to be born again (John 16: 7, 11).

After being born again, the Holy Spirit will then teach you the atoning work of Christ, the death and resurrection, the virgin birth which your earthly and natural wisdom will not understand. God wants us to seek Him to understand His supernatural power. He wants to teach us His ways and His will. He wants to use us within the supernatural to transform communities and nations including those who teach within the school. God wants to teach them the importance of the knowledge of Him in educating the end time personnel. Education begins in the garden of Eden, but it was being high jacked by the devil who corrupts the entire education system where he began to teach man about lies and deception.

A doctor studies the function of man's body and how to sustain him and bring healing. But now, it is no longer about sustaining man but about making billions of dollars. If you are sick in this time, without money, you may die without getting medical help, because it is all about the money. It is the same way with lawyers, they are the ones to teach us about knowledge but Jesus said they hid the key – they hold back from teaching the people.

It is not God's intention for man to suffer, but because of greed and the lack of knowledge of the things of God, many are dying. That is why God will raise up people in the end time and unlock the mystery and the solution to bring change in every sector. He will begin to show people the supernatural way to bringing healing and deliverance. He will show them the purpose of the fruits and the plants, the mystery of the things that He created like simple things in our midst to bring cure. Then man will begin to trust God again to bring growth to their economy. Man will begin to have faith in God.

It is surprising that many who says they are Christians does not believe in the supernatural. There are benefits to be a Christian. The natural things are just for the world, they cannot go beyond the supernatural. It is time for us to accept Him and reconnect and be restored, renewed, recover what is lost. We must understand that prayer, praise and worship, giving, God's grace, God's favor, salvation, love and righteousness brings us in the supernatural.

Shifting Winds

The wind has shifted! When the wind shifts, it affects everything - authority, priority, as well as political and military direction and market conditions. If we - whether individually or collectively - don't shift with the shift then, we will be shifted out and there will be great losses, not profits.

When the wind shifts, even an aircraft has to change direction in order to continue safely and avoid crashing. It is called 'wind shear'. In weather, a 'wind shear' is a microscale meteorological phenomenon occurring over a very small distance. So we are in an unpredictable time, where the seasons are irregular, and so, where there was once predictability and comfortability, those no longer exists. So many have plans - whether to go to war or gain power at any level - but only God's plan will be accomplished. As a result, we now have to change the runway we use in order to safely get off the ground.

Things will become so serious that even famous and historical landmarks will be utterly destroyed. So if people don't change the way they think and operate, we will see the suicide rate increase to a level we have never seen before.

The Truth About Storms

Jonah 1: 4 - 5 says, "But the Lord sent out a great wind on the sea, and there was a mighty tempest on the sea, so that the ship was about to be broken up. Then the mariners were afraid; and every man cried out to his god, and threw the cargo that was in the ship into the sea, to lighten the load.[a] But Jonah had gone down into the lowest parts of the ship, had lain down, and was fast asleep."

There are many debates about storms, hurricanes etc. According to the Webster's New College Dictionary, a *"tempest"* is "a violent storm with high winds, especially one accompanied by rain, hail or snow."

Storms come in many ways. There are storms of life that God speaks to us about in Psalm 46 and He lets us know that He is ever present in our time of trouble. We have storms to test the measure of our faith and Jesus said in the Scriptures "O ye of little faith..."

Storms cleanse the earth, purge, removes old things and brings new things to the forefront. It uproots trees and even blows seeds to new places. Storms can even create jobs for the poor. Storms reveal the hearts of those in leadership and whether or not they truly care for the people and are willing to offer assistance in times of disaster.

There are contrary winds which oppose God's will for your life. We see it in the Scriptures when the disciples were crossing over and there were contrary winds that Jesus rebuked.

In Matthew 14: 22 - 33 Jesus knew that the contrary wind was coming and furthermore He wanted to see if they were ready to go to the next level in the supernatural. He also wanted to show His humanity and reveal His Deity and power over the elements which He created. (Read Luke 8: 35; Mark 4: 39)

Storms also promote some and bring others to repentance. There are many Scriptures which tell us that God rides on the very wind. God speaks through nature and each person may receive a different message. Storms change priorities, mandates and motives. Storms also speak to us about apocalyptic happenings and things to come. (Luke 21; Revelation 6 - which are coming).

Each person has a message. But what stood out to me is Jonah 1: 4 where God sent a great wind on the sea - a mighty tempest. This could possibly be a category 5 hurricane because it threatened to break up a ship. This came about because of Jonah's disobedience because Jonah was running from the presence of God. He did not want to go and preach repentance to the people to whom God wanted to show mercy.

So, the question is, could it be that storms are coming up because of the disobedience of some of God's people who no longer want to preach repentance and have gone in a different direction doing their own thing? In the midst of all that Jonah was fast asleep in the midst of the boatful of people worshipping other gods. Jonah didn't even want to identify himself as a prophet of God until his life was threatened and he had no choice. Is that what it will take for the prophets of God to do what God says? In all of it, Jonah asked to be thrown overboard because He knew that it was him and his disobedience that brought on the storm. It is after that we see the transformation take place with those aboard the ship. So the Holy Spirit said to me - the storm preached the gospel that Jonah would not! So when men in different nations throughout the globe stop preaching the gospel and compromise, He will use nature to preach just as in the days of Noah. And it will not just threaten the lives of the saved but also the unsaved. We will see many disasters globally unless we preach the gospel.

Those governments and organizations who refuse to change direction and refuse to help the poor the fatherless and the widow and refuse to embrace Godly environment and principles will end up 'shipwrecked' and will spend far more than they bargained for to recover from natural disasters.

When we fail to listen to God's true servants, then we will have to listen to the wind and nature that don't need permission, regulations or visas and cannot be sanctioned, regulated or zoned.

The Contrary Wind

There are five main types of wind in the Bible - each having a different purpose.

Remember that the wind symbolizes the regenerative work of the Spirit of God and it is indicative of His mysterious, penetrating, life-giving and purifying operation.

Now there is also a type of Contrary Wind (Mark 6) which brings confusion, deception, opposition by the enemy, fear, lies and fights against your purpose and your assignment. That wind comes from the enemy.

Distraction brings deception. Don't be distracted in this season, focus on the Holy Spirit in this season. There are rough times ahead. This is the time for the unsaved and the backsliders to come home.

We do not walk by sight, we walk by faith! Don't look at what you see, because what you see, may not be what you think it is. Backsliders! Sinners! Time's up!

We are in a time where the East Wind, West Wind and the Contrary winds are blowing.

Discerning The Wind

We have seen different winds blowing since particularly since the beginning of the COVID-19 pandemic; but there are different kinds of winds, and it is critical for us to know which wind is blowing in this season in order to make the proper strategic plans – economically, politically and otherwise. In addition to that, recognize that there are contrary winds which is not God's will and they come with death and deception. The current UN Secretary General also stated recently that there is "a wind of madness is sweeping the globe" and he is quite right.

The Scriptures speak about the four winds in the end times, and they are critical to the Apocalyptic events that would take place in the end-time. These four winds also play a part in Ezekiel 37.

The Hebrew word for the word "Wind" is *"Ruach"* and the Greek word is *"Pneuma"* which further means *"Spirit and Breath"*. Christ illustrates the working of the Holy Spirit in regeneration. John 3: 8 says, "The wind blows where it wishes, and you hear the sound of it, but cannot tell where it comes from and where it goes. So is everyone who is born of the Spirit." God uses the wind as an instrument to carry out His pleasure and His judgement.

Each time something new is going to happen within a nation – a wind blows. It could be a wind of change. If it is a contrary wind, then that is the enemy. There are prophecies and prayers which positively affect the wind. In Ezekiel 37, God instructed the prophet to begin prophesying (not preaching) to the dry bones – those who were hopeless, in exile and cursed; those in suffering, debt and were without hope. He was to declare that there be order and a spiritual regeneration/birthing, resurrection and restoration to take place. Without the Holy Spirit functioning within nations, Administrations, there won't be any change nor peace, only total madness, as the UN Secretary General has said.

Leaders globally are fighting for power; some want to be supreme and most are focusing on the wrong thing, while the poor the fatherless and the widow are dying with no one to take care of them.

Without the Holy Spirit, there is no life – in us, in church, in any organization. Whether church, government or any other organization, if we don't embrace the Holy Spirit, Prayer and Prophecy, then we are embracing death. God rules in all nations.

The East Wind

Discerning the wind is critical. We are now seeing an East Wind on the horizon. The East Wind is a dangerous, fierce, rough wind. It plays 2 roles – purging and perishing, and as a result some people get favor and others are forsaken and flushed out. (Jeremiah 18: 17). The east wind can also scatter, sweep and bring calamity upon nations, such as swarms of insects attacking agricultural produce and the farming industry. It also brings famine.

The UN warns that "Billions of desert locusts in East Africa are swarming at "unprecedented numbers" and pose a huge threat to the region's food insecurity." There are news reports that "The swarms are so bad that Somalia declared a national emergency. Ethiopia and Kenya are struggling to maintain the plague, and scientists fear that the insects could spread across Southwest Asia and the Middle East."

The East Wind has the capacity to affect the waters causing cyclones, brining heavy rains that accelerate the breeding of locusts and other invasive insects and destroy crops. This wind scatters and scorches – turning rivers, waters into dry land and dust.

The East Wind is about to blow through nations and it carries with it judgement and brings the destruction of the ship, crew, crops and also brings drought, scorching, scattering, wars and riots. It affects the environment negatively through storms, locusts as well as other plagues and disease. It brings confusion and chaos. (Read Ezekiel 27: 26; Exodus 10: 13, Jonah 4: 8, Exodus 14: 21; Job 27: 21, Isaiah 27: 8, Psalm 78: 26)

The North Wind

Proverbs 25: 23a says "The north wind brings forth rain...", and Jeremiah 1: 13 – 17 lets us know that this wind also brings a whirlwind, a great cloud with raging fire, and that calamity will also break forth from the North.

So, we must watch all the activities that are about to take place within the North – including war. We also need to watch the countries that are North of the equator and discern the happenings, including Israel and the Euphrates River.

Recognize that in order to understand the times and seasons and how to get our inheritance, it is critical for us to discern the wind that is blowing so that we can be ahead.

Revelation Of The End Time

Revelation 13: 13 - 17 "And it performed great signs, even causing fire to come down from heaven to the earth in full view of the people. Because of the signs it was given power to perform on behalf of the first beast, it deceived the inhabitants of the earth. It ordered them to set up an image in honor of the beast who was wounded by the sword and yet lived. The second beast was given power to give breath to the image of the first beast, so that the image could speak and cause all who refused to worship the image to be killed. It also forced all people, great and small, rich and poor, free and slave, to receive a mark on their right hands or on their foreheads, so that they could not buy or sell unless they had the mark, which is the name of the beast or the number of its name."

It is critical for each of us to understand the significance of one's hand and forehead. The "hand" symbolizes honor, service, dedication and allegiance. It also represents contracts, and agreement made. The forehead signifies that which is prominent and determines the identity of something or someone.

In addition to this, recognize that where this scripture speaks of the image was set up and given life, by the enemy of souls, that was mimicking that God did in Genesis 1: 26 - 28 where God made US in His image and gave us life. Anything or anyone made in the image of its creator reflects its creator, so if someone is modified to reflect a different image, they have yielded over their patent to the new image maker.

Whoever owns the patent, owns the image. Whose image do you bear?

God made us perfect, our DNA - perfect.

No Middle Ground

In the end time there will be no middle ground - you are either FOR Christ or ANTI-Christ. Whomever you pledge your allegiance to will be your master, and you cannot say you believe in Christ but don't trust Him to protect you or heal you from a virus. Hence, anyone who comes with anything else and says it is the only way to go back to normal is not only deceived, but they are a part of the anti-Christ system and plan. 1 John 2: 18 says "Dear children, this is the last hour; and as you have heard that the antichrist is coming, even now many antichrists have come. This is how we know it is the last hour."

Christians, be careful! Revelation 16: 2 reminds us of what will happen, "And the first went, and poured out his vial upon the earth; and there fell a noisome and grievous sore upon the men which had the mark of the beast, and upon them which worshipped his image."

Read the Word of God with understanding also. The 666 of which the Bible speaks is not necessarily about a number, but what the number represents. The number 6 signifies image, man, flesh, sin, idol, likeness, carnality and pride. Look at what King Nebuchadnezzar did in Daniel 3: 1.

Know that God made us in *His* image, but He did not give us authorization to make images. (Exodus 20: 4)

Vaccinate yourself with the Blood of Jesus (Dose # 1) and The Word of God (Dose # 2)!

Chapter 15

FAMINE AND NATION-BUILDING

The success of every nation is determined by what they used to build the nation. King Solomon's success resulted from the fact that he didn't just focus on building his house – the central government – but also focused on building God's house. It is not just a physical house, but the establishment of laws that glorified God. (1 Kings 9: 10) The building of God's house is never secondary and the economy of a nation should never affect the building of God's house. Different nations have been building, but on what are they building? With what specifications are they building? Furthermore, to whom are they building? Which house are they building?

Building has to do with policies, laws, implementation methods, philosophies – similar to what we see in Genesis 11 where they wanted to build a global economic system without God's input or involvement. They were building God out of their plans and systems. They wanted the blessings of God without God, hence, as a result, it brought chaos and downfall, famine, starvation, global migration and brain drain.

When we build God's House He will build our house. Solomon understood and that is why he surpassed all the kings of the earth during his time, in riches and wealth. (1 Kings 12: 24)

Abortion and Nation-Building

Recently we saw a law being passed in New York to legalize the abortion of babies even up to full term; and the Trade Center was lit up in celebration. That is building as well, but building to what and with what? And what will the reward be? Abortion does not happen in a vacuum, it is also the abortion of futures, nations and economies as well and bring famine. So many third world nations – including Jamaica – are utilizing this building principle to build their nation. Are they willing to deal with the consequences of that? They need to remember that the chairman – the Sovereign, Supreme One have both veto power and the power to override laws, treaties, and resolutions (binding and non-binding).

It is so disappointing to see young politicians simply abort their political future by supporting abortion to build nations.

Famine

Every person within each nation needs to know that the actions of past administrations affect present administrations. So even when new leaders are installed, they are often blamed for the misdirection of the nation caused by the actions of the past administrations. Recognize that unless there is atonement and restitution, the effects of the action does not simply disappear, and when harvest comes, then those effects will birth out famine!

The Oxford dictionary defines famine as "extreme scarcity of food; starvation". From a Biblical perspective, famine always comes to get the people back to God. It also promotes the true leaders. We have famine where there is war, crime, and violence on the increase. Famine for food, caused by drought and it triggers price increases and food shortage. It affects livestock and agriculture in general.

There is also the famine that is the result of economic systems crashing – recession, foreclosures, receiverships and massive murders are the result. However, the most dangerous one happens when God goes silent on a nation.

Preparation and Planning

We are in a time now where planning, preparation, positioning and stockpiling are the keys for survival. Nobody wants to be in a situation where the money we have become so greedy for becomes valueless, or to get to the stage where someone would be willing to give away their livestock and land just to get bread and water for survival.

In a famine, those who have food will always have power. So if food and water be the order of the day, what will become of the stock market and the money we fought so hard to hoard?

Famine will also level the economic field, where economic equality results and everyone will be on the same level financially.

Famine tests every individual's foundation and also the foundation used to build and reveal true advisors are and who are not.

My advice is that each person take up their responsibility to have a plan in place for themselves and their family for survival, because when the dust settles at the end of the day it will be every man for himself and loyalty will by a rare thing. The highest bidder will win.

Famine, Farming And Faith

The globe has been taking serious hits in the area of agriculture. Some time ago the Australian fires destroyed 1 billion animals either as a direct result of the fire or from related causes, such as starvation, dehydration or habitat loss. Furthermore, more than 2 million wild animals died in the Bolivian wildfires and the damage is said to be irreversible. In Bolivia in particular, the fires have so far destroyed more than 4.9 million acres of forest in one of South America's key regions for cat wildlife, which has the highest predicted density of cat species on the continent.

Highly regarded international Organizations have stated that, "Poorer countries with rising populations and scarce natural resources are likely to be "increasingly dependent" on imports to feed their people"

What is happening globally, coupled with the pending disasters that will undoubtedly affect Agriculture worldwide, lets us know that we are on the course of a famine, which would also trigger an economic recession. Farming and Agriculture should be the number one priority of any and every nation today – particularly for the African and Caribbean Regions. It therefore means that the country which controls food and food supply will become "king". It is similar to what transpired in the Bible when Egypt became the food hub of the region and all nations, including Israel had to travel to Egypt to purchase food. Everything else became secondary. Not many will care about the stock market, tourism or gender rights when that happens, because when a man is hungry, when a person sees their children hungry, priorities are re-aligned.

Farmers in poorer countries have been getting terrible hits and most are turning away from the industry as there is little support for them. The FAO documented that 83 per cent of all drought-caused economic losses, that is $29 billion, were absorbed by agriculture. In addition to this, between 2005 and 2015 natural disasters cost the agricultural sectors of developing country economies a staggering $96 billion in damaged or lost crop and livestock production, $48 billion of which occurred in Asia. What could it be as of today?

Urgent Action Needed

Any country that deals with this crisis-level situation as a priority and puts farming at the top of their list of strategies to employ, they will benefit significantly and save their nation from starvation. Nations must focus on two main areas of farming, commercial and subsistence.

Possible solutions include:

- ✓ Land Freeze. Cease all divestment of land and building in certain areas; and instead farm those lands.

- ✓ Build Warehouses for storage of food and other necessary items.

- ✓ Grant cheap loans to Farmers to facilitate purchase of equipment and machinery for farming, livestock and the preservation of crops.

- ✓ Encourage the poor to purchase deep freezers so they can store seafood, meats and vegetables.

- ✓ Store water and ensure that storage in plastic containers is avoided.

- ✓ Invest more in fresh water fish.

- ✓ Poorer families must begin to plant all vegetables, melon, scallion, yams, corn and potatoes – not just for survival, but they must find ways to convert these items. For example, turning corn into cornmeal.

- ✓ More people need to in rearing more goats, pigs and chickens. They must also find creative ways to preserve these meats.

- ✓ Farmers must learn Biblical Principles for successful farming – the Law of Gleaning.

- ✓ Dig more wells.

Faith

Famine, Farming and Faith are all connected. There cannot be successful farming if God is not in it. It is the oldest and foremost profession in the Bible. We must have faith in God that what He says we are to do in order to survive and be successful is what is needed and then do it. We have already seen the results of losing the sugar cane, banana industries and how other crops have succumbed to various diseases. In order not to fall into conspiracy theories as speculated, we must revert to our original fertilizers, rather then the modern ones. We must protect our soil. Furthermore, climate change has its place, but not as it has been presented to the public. We have the authority to create our environment.

Let us prepare.

Prepare For Revival

Revival is a word that many speak about and many desire to see. But revival does not necessarily come the way we think it should. For example, many often think revival is about miracles happening all at once or signs and wonders manifesting. Meanwhile, others think it is another opportunity for "prophets" to fleece some people. But that's not it.

In the true sense of the word, a revival indicates that something has been restored or has come to life again. It means an improvement in the condition or strength of something. It also means an instance of something becoming popular, active, or important again; a reawakening of religious fervor – where souls are being saved or there is a major outpouring of God's Presence in the earth. It is important to note that a revival can often be started by an adverse occurrence. For example, the COVID-19 Pandemic is an adverse occurrence, however, it has started a revival within the Church, bringing them back to basics and restoring proper priorities. The Caribbean is on the verge of revival because of what is about to take place in the region in many areas. This will bring the latter rain which will cause revival.

How To Cause Revival

There has to be a build up of prayer, fasting, giving, declaration, worship, travailing, evangelism and holiness. This will create an environment for the Holy Spirit to move freely. Revival comes through pressure and is like a reset. The dormant thing will come back to life; there will no longer be a desire for sin, divination, kundalini spirit, and the demolition of the Jezebel spirit. The counterfeit will be broken and the genuine and authentic will emerge. Jesus will become the center of the people again. The eyes of the people will be opened to truth; the zeal for the house of God will return. Man's hope and trust will be in God again and not in politicians and scientists.

Foundation Shaken

In a revival, we will begin to see the shaking of foundations. Similarly, when Peter, Paul and Silas were "released" from prison through the shaking of the earthquake, that was a revival. (Acts 3; Joel 2: 28 – 29) A time of refreshing and the return of the backsliders. Looking at the outpouring of the Holy Spirit in the Upper Room found in the Book of Acts, we see the Law of Multiplication occurring – signs and wonders, growth, increase, healing and deliverance. When the persecution of the saints were taking place in the book of Acts, many were losing their jobs, a unity came about through the Holy Spirit. Many began to give without limitation and lay things at the Apostles' feet for distribution to those who were not working. There was no lack. It happened already and it will happen again.

Revival In The Family

There will be a revival in the family. The pouring out of the Malachi 4: 5 – 6 Anointing for the restoration of families, particularly between children and their fathers. This revival will destroy the gender agenda that many are using to divide the family.

We are about to see husbands and wives serve God together again in the house of the Lord, according to Ephesians 5, where husbands will "sanctify and cleanse her (the wife) with the washing of water by the word".

Revival In The Marketplace

The deceptive market strategies are about to come to an end. Famine, recession. This will open the door for Biblical and Kingdom Economics, where Godly principles will be accepted and established within the marketplace, and only those organizations that accept it will survive.

Prayer will return to the workplace, to the schools and to the prisons.

Darkness will begin to disappear and righteous leaders will begin to emerge.

We will begin to see the alignment and proper functioning of the luminary bodies; and a reduction of lies about climate change – the Glory of God will manifest! Ezekiel 47 and Revelation 22 will begin to take place.

There will be healing of nations by the pouring out of God's Spirit, where the poor the fatherless and the widow will be taken care of by the Government of God in the earth – His Church. There will be fair distribution of resources.

We will see the manifestation of the Holy Spirit in different forms.

- ✓ The Dove symbolizing peace, power, patience and purity.
- ✓ The Oil symbolizing purity and health;
- ✓ The Water symbolizing the cleansing;
- ✓ The Wind symbolizing the regenerative work of the Holy Spirit; and
- ✓ The Seal symbolizing ownership and authority.

Prepare for the revival!

Preparing For The Famine

The pandemic we are currently facing is indeed a more than a cause for great concern, but what is even more threatening to the globe is the path the word is currently on toward a famine of Biblical proportions.

While different regions are experiencing different plagues and disasters, it is just a matter of time before everything culminates impacting the globe significantly. The famine will include more unemployment, drought, crime, violence, wars, disasters, financial recession, plagues and pandemics.

Up to 2018, UNICEF reported that conflict, drought, displacement and disease drove massive humanitarian crises, causing 20 million people to be at risk of famine across Yemen, Somalia, South Sudan and north-east Nigeria – including nearly 1.3 million severely malnourished children at imminent risk of death.

Further to this, UN humanitarian chief Mark Lowcock said, in an interview, that the economic fallout from the pandemic including lock downs, border closures and restrictions on movement have all had a big effect on food security and agricultural productivity. And extremists have taken the opportunity to make hay out of all this, he said.

"Everybody is very preoccupied by COVID and the virus," Lowcock said. But "it is not the virus that's creating most of the carnage. It is other things, and we need to focus on the things that will really cause the biggest loss of life."

The Trouble Ahead

While many countries have great hopes of recovering from COVID-19, there needs to be preparation for greater problems ahead. For example, the shortage of food and water as well as price hikes, and stock market instability. We are already seeing riots and looting taking place in different countries including the United States of America (USA). With the US Elections pending, we may see further crises which have the potential to affect food security. I also believe there is going to be a run on the banks, and some banks will be closing their doors, and that will be an even greater problem for those who do not own a bank card, particularly the senior citizens.

While some governments encourage the people to pay their bills online, what would happen if banks begin to go under, or minimize the amount you can use or collect on a daily basis.

Oil Shortage

There are proposed oil shortages ahead, and that will increase food and energy costs which will cause some economies to spiral downward. So, it is critical for poorer nations to find alternative sources of energy to survive.

Solutions

Nations need to:

Identify the old riverbeds and courses that have been 'developed' and built on and pull out of those areas. There needs to be intensive 'river training' activities and building of protective walls. More dams need to be built. Food storage must be implemented at both individual and national levels to prevent price gouging, which will lead to famine and starvation. Keep cash on hand, and don't put all your money in one financial institution.

Coordinate with churches and other non-governmental organizations to provide support to deal with the spiritual needs of the people. Oftentimes, there is great focus on providing food and other physical amenities, but no attention is given to the mental and emotional toll that disasters have on individuals and as a result, that aspect is neglected.

Know That:

Serious problems with weather patterns will continue. Tsunamis, earthquakes, flooding, fire, and hailstones will occur. Most geographical areas and landscapes will change. Environmental problems will increase. Food and water will be contaminated because of the high level of activities within the ocean. The fish are not safe, and there needs to be major testing.

There is good and bad that can be found in the midst of a famine, however. Nations and organizations that are properly prepared always have an advantage and will have dominion in times of famine. Stockpiling and logistics are key in moving forward.

The question then becomes, "Is there enough food, medication or water available globally to deal with a global famine?

Great Faith In Famine

Unless there is global repentance and Divine Intervention, we are going to walk the path of great famine. There are many instances of famine mentioned in history. The famine of 1769, The Bengal Famine, The Irish Famine of

1845, The Famine of China in 1878 were some which cause a great death toll. With the pandemic and bad decisions made by the global leaders, the globe is being pushed on a path of famine.

Amos 8: 11 – 12 says, ""Behold, the days are coming," says the Lord God, "That I will send a famine on the land, Not a famine of bread, Nor a thirst for water, But of hearing the words of the Lord. They shall wander from sea to sea, And from north to east; They shall run to and fro, seeking the word of the Lord, But shall not find it."

The Basis of The Famine

Famine and drought were two (2) of the punishments God used against His people. The Book of Amos speaks of a new kind of famine – the famine for the Word of God, which brings serious repercussions. Solutions from the Word of the Lord will be very rare. Man has been trying to silence the truth and they will pay the price – they will be plundered. When God is silent (because man refuses to listen), man will try to silence the truth and will pay the consequences. We are now seeing blatant censorship taking place in the media.

Scientists are now failing badly because nothing they are trying to do is working.

There are different types of famines mentioned in the Bible – disaster, drought, crop failure, locusts and viruses, war and natural calamity, price increases – and all these are already happening. It will take great faith for people to deal with it.

While famine alignment and reset spiritually and naturally, and brings change in the earth, it also allows us to move away from Moab. So, while many are trying to prevent migration, the famine ahead will be so severe that there will be increased migration as people seek for survival. People will be going to and fro. That is why, countries who try to close their borders from the poor will be affected severely. The Law of Gleaning (Leviticus 23: 20 – 22) must be practiced, if companies and countries are going to stand.

End-Time Happenings

Famine also depicts end-time happenings and has to do with government mis-management and bad policies, wrong economic priorities, and a lack of policies regarding farming.

Many companies and nations are focusing on digital currency, bitcoins, the Metaverse, and AI (Artificial Intelligence) among other things. What use will any of this have when people are dying of hunger?

Price increases, lack of employment opportunities, loss of employment, cause famine and lead to malnutrition and the lack of basic needs, and all this is already rampant in our world now.

Many also think that over-population is the cause of famine. That is not true and that thought should never be entertained. Lack of proper stewardship by leaders, and political mismanagement are the main reasons for famine.

Renew Your Mind

For the faithful ones, in order to deal with famine their minds must be renewed. We must look to God as our Source; and look to Him for our increase, just as was done with the 5 loaves and 2 fishes. We must also look to receive blessings from unknown places and unknown people.

In 2 Kings 4: 38 – 44, there was a man from *Baal Shalisha*, who came to bless him. It was a place where they worshipped other gods not the True and Living God; and he came to bless the prophet of God.

God always blesses His people from the "muddy places". We have to follow instruction and be satisfied with God's provision that He has made for His people. We MUST live by the Word to get wealth – the undiluted word, not false prosperity. We must be led by the Holy Spirit to bring us through, that we can deal with the problems ahead. In addition to this, the type of doctrine we embrace is critical to our survival.

It is also critical for certain nations to remove certain taxes and regulations from certain basic items. Nations must stockpile food and medication now. Any country that has food will have power. Serious contingency plans must be put in place for the poor.

The Just must live by faith!

Chapter 16

THE GANGS, THE GATES, AND THE POWER OF MUSIC

Gangs And The Power Of Music

Crime seems to be the order of the day, especially gang activity. We have seen over the years that we cannot truly deal with crime until we deal with the root and cause of the issue. There are many experts on crime but all they are doing is making noise.

Have you ever taken the time to notice that many of these gang leaders are true leaders – they have the gift of leadership. Recognize that most often, where the problems lie, there lies the solution also. So, many of them have the solutions to the problems we see. Therefore, the focus should be to target gang leaders, restore them and utilize them and their skills in addressing the issues affecting the communities.

Societal Influence on Gang Leaders

In dealing with gang leaders, we should look at the story of Jephthah in Judges 11, he was forced to be a gang leader by others who see themselves as worthless/hopeless within the society. They were looking for love, acceptance, leadership and possible fathering/mentoring, so they drew to Jephthah who had suffered injustices, classism and rejection. He was thrown out of his inheritance because of how he was conceived – his mother was a prostitute. Many within society today would say "abort" him. What we need to recognize is that the very thing we want to reject and to kill is often what God has sent to help us in the first place. Every soul has a purpose and an assignment.

Jephthah's becoming a gang leader was the result of society's treatment toward him. Understand also, that like-minded people will come together; just as the rich stick to those of their own income bracket, those with similar life experiences do that as well.

Jephthah's assignment was to save the nation and to become the military and civil leader for the nation. He was able to solve a problem that the then leaders could not solve.

No politician or military personnel can change the nation, only a new heart can bring change. That is why our prisons should be a place of genuine rehabilitation, not a place were people go in and come out worse than they went in. More funding needs to be directed toward rehabilitation programs for prisoners. There is the great need for Spirit-filled Chaplains, not yoga practitioners in the process of rehabilitation. The Gospel of Jesus Christ is the catalyst for real change. Furthermore, prison is the best place for intelligence gathering; you would be surprised what many gang leaders know.

Rehabilitation: What's The Focus

In dealing with gangs, we cannot focus only on the men, but we need to concentrate also on the women behind them. We need to target the market, the product and the funding behind it all. We must bind the strongman over each area they operate. There is always a strongman over an area and behind the problems.

We must also examine the various reasons people enter gangs – profit, fame employment, acceptance, love and power.

We need more "At-Risk" Programs, Mentorship, and set better mentors, skills training opportunities and teach them to dress and protocol.
Politicians also need to be truthful, because many of them use the gangs to maintain power so they don't want the gangs dismantled. It's just a matter of time before the gangs and their leaders turn against such politicians in a way they will not expect.

The Sound of Music

Sound, music is a critical tool to dismantle and change gang leaders; particularly those within crime. Sounds affect mood, anxiety levels and has significant psychological effects. It can impact they brain and a person's way of thinking.

It is no secret that many rich people listen mainly Classical Music, as well as Jazz, Blues, and Opera. The organ, flute and harp were instruments that were used to bring peace and to boost low testosterone levels and sex drive. It also elevates serotonin levels in a person – the chemical within the body that promotes feelings of happiness.

So if they were to change the music for one month as a test on a particular area; show love and affection and dress them in jackets/suits (both male and female), we might be surprised at the outcome and the change that would take place among them.

It is critical for us to understand the importance of gates and gatekeepers within a nation particularly in these end times. If we are going to have true reformation and change, then we are going to have to adjust, rebuild and repair. Let us look at the Gatekeepers

Who are the Gate-Keepers

1. Police
2. Soldiers
3. Security Guards
4. Customs
5. Immigration
6. Corrections Staff
7. Church (The Fivefold Personnel – Gatekeepers for spiritual and natural things)
8. Governmental Institution (particularly Finance, Foreign Affairs and Tax Office)

The Gates and Gatekeepers within a nation are important, as they control the access to a city or a nation.

The Gate must be manned, and the Gatekeepers must be taken care of. For example, they should be given incentives such as Tax-free/Tax exemption benefits, to motivate them. (Ezra 2: 42, 2 Chronicles 9: 17 – 22, Isaiah 62: 6 – 10, Nehemiah 11: 19, 1 Chronicles 26: 1 – 2, Nehemiah 3)

Focus on Internal Security

Oftentimes, we focus on internal security but neglect external security. For example, those coming in under the disguise of 'tourist' or ex-patriates and contractors, what are their mandates and motives? What systems are in place to monitor their movements? Are they a part of the negative activities we see daily? Who monitors the contractor and those engineers building the roads? What are they doing?

No gatekeeper can be effective unless we allow God to build.

Psalm 127: 1 says, "Unless the Lord builds the house, they labor in vain who build it; unless the Lord guards the city, the watchman stays awake in vain."

Oftentimes organizations are negative toward God's principles, people and in fact, anything to do with God, including devotions and prayer.

The Gates In A Nation

The Sheep Gate -   The purpose of that gate is ministry to God's people. Teach, Educate, Empower and Feed the people. If the people are not being fed with God's wisdom and knowledge, then we will fail. Furthermore, compassion must be shown. Good leaders – shepherds – must motivate the people. Sheep feed best when they know the shepherd is close by to feed them. They feel secure. (John 10: 2 – 3). Shepherds must not only care about themselves, but they must care about the Sheep. The management is the shepherd, the staff members are the sheep. It is about more than money. The sheep need that personal touch from the shepherd. That is why Pastors have to lay hands on the sheep. A shepherd must be a counselor and must spend time with the sheep.

The Fish Gate -   (Nehemiah 3: 3) This is Ministry to the unsaved. All the gatekeepers are called to minister to the unsaved. One word of encouragement will reduce crime. When the organization begins to create an environment for spiritual empowerment, then we will begin to see change. We must restore the Sheep Gate before the Fish Gate. Healthy sheep will produce healthy lambs through the evangelism. This ministry includes training and equipping. What if all our prisoners began to be equipped Spiritually? A transformation would begin, budgets would be cut and most of them would change and not return to the prisons. So when people go to prison, they should come out rehabilitated not remain the same as they were before or get worse. Only the Gospel of Jesus Christ can bring that about, not New Age practices.

The Old Gate   -   (Nehemiah 3: 6) The purpose of this gate is foundational principles and truths, Moral principles. Truth never changes from Generation to generation. When we try to remove the ancient landmark which our fathers have set, then we will have problems within the nation. So new truths will are coming in with which we have been compromising. For example, doctrine, theology and philosophy, which are not in line with Biblical Principles (Proverbs 22: 28 Proverbs 23: 10, Hebrews 6: 1 – 3, Acts 2: 41 – 42)

The Valley Gate -   (Nehemiah 3: 13) It's purpose is the ministry of compassion. We must always to meet another person's need. Kindness and meekness are mandatory. Helping a fallen brother, who has emotional, financial, mental, domestic challenges must have a support system in place to help staff who are the gatekeepers. This will prevent bribery.

The Dung Gate -   This deals with the ministry of cleansing and so its purpose is to provide the inhabitants of the city with a place where they can dispose their garbage or waste. If there is no place for disposal of waste and garbage and to allow for repentance and change then people will become sick. Sin makes one sick. The Church cannot be exempt from the nation, neither can Christ be excluded from the nation.

The Fountain Gate - This is the Holy Spirit that would bring revival, refreshing and restoration. So when the garbage such as unforgiveness, bitterness and hatred is emptied out of our lives, then the Holy Spirit – Who is the Fountain Gate, will manifest, and we will begin to get solutions, and rivers of water will begin to flow out of the lives of the people, and a time of refreshing (Acts 3: 19 – 21) will take place. The economy will also grow and our borders will be secure. God does nothing without His Spirit. (Zechariah 10: 1, Hosea 6: 3, John 7: 37 – 39, Joel 2). Prayer and praise changes the environment.

The Water Gate - The Ministry of God's Word. Only through God's Word can cleansing take place naturally of spiritually. No nation or individual can survive without water. The Spirit of God moves when the Word of God is declare. Both the Spirit and the Word work together. (Numbers 31: 23, Numbers 33: 9, Deuteronomy 8: 15, 1 Corinthians 10: 4) So, we truly cannot lead without the Word.

The Horse Gate - We need burden-bearers to carry heavy burdens. There are burdens problems that are too difficult to carry. There are some problems man cannot solve. So we need intercessors to continue to pray for God's counsel, will and ways. The carnal man cannot solve the spiritual problems without the Holy Spirit. We can't solve the problems with our intellect and without God. So the burden must be lifted from the flesh to the Spiritual.

The East Gate - This one dictates a final restoration coming. Christ is coming back. There is a perfecting that is taking place now in the Body of Christ. He is coming back for a church without spot or wrinkle, so we must be ready. (Revelation 7: 2, Revelation 16: 12)

Chapter 17

GLOBAL RESET

Many will be hearing about an economic reset. However, when there is a *"global reset"* EVERYTHING is reset! So there will be new desires, new priorities, new currency. We will begin to see a fixed system, a barter system, gold-backed system will come to the fore, and plastic will replace cash. Countries on the peg system which is a policy where the government sets a specific exchange rate for its currency. It will be interesting times.

Things Will Never Be The Same Again

"The normal rules no longer applies ..." (Words of the UN Secretary General, Antonio Guterres). The ILO says, "Workers could lose US$3.4M of income..." Hence, I guarantee that laws, treaties and bi-lateral agreements will change with each nation during this reset.

We must as Christians reset our faith. God must be first in our lives again. (Matthew 6: 33). We cannot be too busy to seek Him anymore. Who you trust for economic stability in this season (individually or nationally) is critical. Jeremiah 17: 7 - 8 is very important to every Christian. If your hope and trust are in God, there is no need to fear in times of global reset. You will prosper and continue to bear fruit with expansion, new ideas, and new strategies.

The Body Of Christ

We need to get back to the true foundation, according to Luke 4: 18 – 19, Matthew 28: 18 – 20 and Ephesians 4: 11. We must also teach the Gospel, the Epistle and the Book of Revelation. Surprisingly, in this transition, I have heard many pastors and prophets referring to the events of the Book of Revelation (which are happening now as fear-driven conspiracy theories, and many of them refuse to teach it. Some don't even read the Book of Revelation. However, we must recognize that if we fail to fully equip the people, then every wind of doctrine with blow them to and fro, and they will not be able to fulfill their purpose. Why don't many pastors teach about the contents of the Book of Revelation? Can anyone live or survive without God's help? Was the Church more focused on buildings and other infrastructure, rather than the state of the souls of those God called them to win? The doctrine that you have been taught, is it supported by the Bible?

Regardless of the reset that is taking place, never forget Revelation 21 especially verses 4 – 5, *"And God will wipe away every tear from their eyes; there shall be no more death, nor sorrow, nor crying. There shall be no more pain, for the former things have passed away. Then He who sat on the throne said, "Behold, I make all things new." And He said to me, "Write, for these words are true and faithful.""*

Seven Areas Of Economic Focus

In order for us to get back to true prosperity and recover from our present economic situation, we must get back to Biblical basics.

The first step is learning about the six (6) main seasons, according to Genesis 8: 22, which are Seedtime (mid-October to mid-December), Winter (mid-December to mid-February), Cold (mid- February to mid-April), Harvest (mid-April to mid-June), Summer (mid-June to mid-August) and Heat (mid-August to mid-October).

Further to this, it is important to know that the Lunar Months are critical to prosperity. A lunar month is the duration between consecutive new moons. (It is also called a lunation or synodic month) is on average of 29 days 12 hours and 44 minutes. In other words, every 29 days, 12 hours and 44 minutes is a lunar/synodic month.

You may ask why this is important to know. Let us look at Seedtime for example. This period of mid-October to mid-December is the best time (but not the only time) to sow. Furthermore, in order to understand when it is Spring – when things begin to spring up again, we would take our cue from the almond tree (Exodus 25: 33 – 36; Jeremiah 1: 11; Genesis 43:11; Numbers 17: 1 – 8). This is a good time for investment.

In addition to the Seasons, those who want to gain and/or maintain wealth, Tithing is the key. The difference between Tithes and Offerings is that the Tithes function like your insurance coverage and though that, new ideas

220

and strategies for operations are downloaded to you. The Offering unlocks earthly material needs or wants.

Many individuals and organizations no longer honor God nor abide by His principles. They, instead, give into unclean works. Most persons depend on their knowledge and expertise without God's input, hence our current economic problems. As a result, the favor of God shifted.

In addition to all this, Tithes need to be paid on behalf of the nation.

Education

We must get back to educating God's way. We have diverted from that and have corrupted our youth. Our education must bring illumination and edification. The Word of God must be the foundation of all we do, especially when it comes to empowering the next generation.

Knowledge originally comes from God, and as such must be pure. We must educate our people to be owners not slaves. We must educate our people to function within their gifts. Not everyone was created to be a doctor or a lawyer. Some will be landowners and farmers, others will be musicians, oil drillers, teachers. We must seek to embrace more of the Montessori approach to learning. Furthermore, we must revisit the matter of Free Education and bring it to fruition. This will help us to achieve the Sustainable Development Goals of 2030, and also address the current problems that exist such as food insecurity, health and make way for botanists, marine biologists and much more.

Family

We need to teach our people proper parenting from a scriptural perspective. Furthermore, a Ministry of Family Affairs needs to be established within the nation. More counseling Centers are needed for the family as the first line of government.

Shelter

This will be a very important area in which to invest, because there will be serious challenges ahead. The surge in unemployment will cause many to be homeless and solutions will be needed. We will need to look at temporary housing, and waive property taxes for the next two (2) years.

Food Banks

Nations need to set up Food Banks to deal with the famine ahead, and reduce Sales Tax (such as 10% GCT and VAT) on all taxed items.

Health

There needs to be overall reduction in the cost of medicines, particularly those for diabetes, asthma, and children's medication. More clinics and research centers need to be set up. More research of our plants and fruits need to be carried out. There must also be training for community nurses as well as the stockpiling of vaccines and other medical supplies.

Agriculture

The farmers need to be heard. They need to have financial assistance concerning their farms, and the need for that will become visibly significant within the next **ten (10) months**. Stockpiling seeds and reduction in the cost of farming equipment are key. Increase community farming and making it a part of the school curriculum is vital.

Global Shift And Harvest

Most of the happenings worldwide have shown us the failure of the leaders at various levels throughout the globe to deal with the needs of the people. Many are starving because of the policies imposed during the COVID-19 Pandemic – and this as a result of the fact that leaders fail to seek and listen to God in building. So instead, they continue to build on sand. (Psalm 127; Matthew 7). 1 Corinthians 7: 13 – 14 clearly outlines the solutions in times of problem.

Shifting And Shaking

Our global leaders hastily embrace the anti-Christ resources that brings nations further into bondage and famine and ultimately affect the sovereignty of most nations. As the global shifting and shaking continues, we will continue to see the relocating and restructuring of families for Kingdom purposes. It is critical for God's people to be sensitive to His move and move with His Spirit. It is a season for the renewal of the mind. The blessings of each person will be tied to the Kingdom. God is about to judge the marine kingdom and pride will be shaken.

Harvest

Matthew 13: 24 – 30 tells us that we are in a time of one of the greatest harvests. In this current harvest we see the wheat and the tears being separated. We are also seeing the manifestation of the five wise and five foolish virgins.

The Bible speaks of many harvests including the harvest of souls, the harvest of miracles and rewards for one's deeds, and the harvest of finance.

We must recognize that during a harvest, we will need to work double time. In harvest time, there will be wars, because the enemy wants to steal our harvest. So, it is critical for us to continue to plant, reap and store. In reaping, we receive some thirty, some sixty, and some a hundred-fold. We are moving into the manifestation of the thousand and ten thousand-fold.

Harvest is something for which we have to prepare. Many believe that the harvest will simply fall into their laps. A person must have faith in order to reap during the harvest season. A farmer does not necessarily wait for perfect weather to plant, he plants regardless of what weather as long as it is within the right season. (Ecclesiastes 3) We don't go according to the world's ways, whether good or bad. The way of the world is finished.

Know The Season of Your Harvest

Every farmer needs to know the season – when to check the maturity of the harvest. In order to do that, there are some things we need to understand about the maturity of the harvest.

When something is mature/ripe, you can see it, feel it, smell it and it sometimes falls from the tree. It has a specific color when it is mature. We must ensure that we do everything to protect our harvest. We must not complain because that kills the harvest. Tithing must continue during the harvest. It protects the harvest. Your tithing is your best pest controller. Many will come to swipe the harvest, but your tithing will rebuke the devourer for your sake. It will also open the windows of heaven and send rain. It will stop predial larceny.

Remember, in times of harvest, we must allow the Lord to lead the reaping. There will be wheat and tares, so there will be exposure during the harvest. God is the One who will root out the false and the fake. The tares can be false doctrines, false teachers, the Judases, the enemies, the goat and only God has the wisdom to do the uprooting. There are many times people will be in your vineyard as a sleeper/undercover, and only God is able to deal with them. So, we must pray to ask Him to purge and protect the vineyard.

We must have high expectations and patience during harvest. Many have sowed and toiled but this is the time of harvest. It can be your healing, the mending of some relationships and restoration. It can also be babies being born, gifts and talents coming forth; promotions, favor for the starting of your business, honor and reward for the good work you have been doing over the years.

This is the time of harvest for you!

Russia, Ukraine And What Is At Stake

The current conflict between Russian and Ukraine has opened the door for many things to happen. First of all it is not surprising as this is the Shemita year; this is the year that there will be a shaking of empires.

The Fight For Superpower Status

The division between the Democrats and the Republicans in the USA has leveled the playing field, and many Western nations now have the opportunity to become the global leader of the West. These nations also have the ambition to become the most militarily dominant nation. They also want to replace the US Dollar and become a global economic superpower – Russia, China and many others are at the top of the heap.

Americans have spent a great deal of time trying to destroy each other from within. America has trampled on the grace God has given them to be the Superpower they have become; however, they have been infiltrated by the Babylonians. They have adopted the Babylonian lifestyle and have exchanged God for Ba'al. If American is to remain on top, then it is critical for them to rebuild the broken altars. They must repent for abortion, racism, classism, and every other kind of prejudice and division in which the people of the nation have been engaged into date.

The Bear and The Dragon

While Russia and China are uniting to compete against America, it is critical for one to understand that a Bear and a Dragon cannot dwell together. While the Bear and the Dragon compete against the Eagle for the spoils and the resources, there is also a major underlying fight to change political and psychological ideologies at the same time.

If you take a good look at what is happening these days, you will see evidence of socialism dressed as capitalism taking the forefront. There is also a plan to weaken the Trans-Atlantic Partnership.

Ideological Changes

Both the Bear and the Dragon have capitalist economies, but a communist/socialist leadership structure. There are many who believe that the West has too much democracy. What this means for us, is that the threats against Christianity will not only increase, but may even be put into action. So, the Anti-Christ system will expand with a view to eradicating Christianity. Within Socialism, there is only the Marxist ideology, which means that God has no place in any aspect of society and religious freedoms and liberty would be at stake. So simply put, the God of the Universe is on trial. Christians must now engage in serious Spiritual Warfare. We must recognize that the pandemic was all about changing our ideologies – a test to see if we were in the position we need to be, in order to allow them to execute their "ideological makeover", and now the war is about cementing that process.

Bondage and Famine

The Western Leaders have been blindfolded for years. Many of these leaders have thought that they could operate from two different platforms. They must return to

God, or else the Babylonian system will put us in bondage and consume them in the process.

Needless to say, it is critical therefore, for God's people to discern the difference between a snake, a cat, a lion, a dragon, a bear, an eagle and a wolf.

If we take a good look, in the height of the pandemic and the war, laws are being passed to remove some of the ancient landmarks as well as other laws that are the foundation of freedoms, and that is why, if we in the West are to survive, we must return to the Lord.

Further to this, the soaring oil prices, skyrocketing food prices as well as the high cost of living, will send many nations into famine.

Pledging Allegiance

It is all about pledging allegiance.

There are benefits offered by both Christ and the Anti-Christ. Whatever choice is made will determine the direction of a nation – whether bondage or liberty. While many allegiances are now being formed, it is critical that people select the right allegiance, because everything else is temporary.

There are reasons for every war, and they come with advantages and disadvantages. For example, some wars are to take over the resources of nations. The disadvantage here is that other enemies to the nation create confusion and more deception to awake sleeping giants that have not gone into war with other nations for a while. So attention will be on, Germany, Japan, China, and Iran, but the target may be on the USA and Israel, based on Biblical Prophecies.

The possible advantage is that Christians have the opportunity to join together to win the lost for Christ. Also, there can be dominion and wealth transfer to the Kingdom, because of the suffering they had endured during the pandemic.

We must pray against any nuclear strike based on Zechariah 14: 12 – 15, and that God will give the Body of Christ more time to set its house in order. We pray that this war does not lead us into World War 3 and fulfill the prophecy of Ezekiel 38.

Capitalizing On Kingdom Economics

The world's way of economics has become obsolete in this era. None of those principles work and modern economists have no solutions and only make statements after the fact. There is a paradigm shift and it is critical for God's people to shift with the shift.

The Kingdom economics principles benefits all if applied by all – regardless of religion, race or any other factors. They work because that is how God intended it to be.

The former way of dealing with losses was to either file for bankruptcy, divest/merge, impose higher taxes on the poor or close. It forces one to borrow from other countries with clauses that have the potential to dictate how already sovereign nations must operate (thereby nullifying the principle of sovereignty) – determining who you should employ, with whom you should do business, who should be in strategic positions in the nation and even determine what percentage should be given to the public sector in wages and some don't go beyond 5%. They will also want to determine your parameters for downsizing in your organization. This is where politicians now become ineffective. Furthermore, they also will want to determine guidelines for our education system and health sector which is anti-Christ.

It is critical if we want to be financially stable and debt-free – whether we are rich or poor – to begin to capitalize on kingdom principles to deal with the challenges ahead, create jobs and move away from this obsolete, deceptive, manipulative spell casting that WILL come to naught.

Keys to Note

The first key and most important key in Kingdom Principles is Daily Obedience to God's instructions. (Deuteronomy 28: 1 – 14)

Learn about Tithing and the various Seasons – particularly the 3 main seasons which will bring us increase. They are March-April – Passover/Resurrection; June – Pentecost; September-October – Tishrei/End and Beginning of Agricultural Season). Remember, the earthly banks only extract from us and give us nothing in return. This will open gates/windows of opportunity, investment strategies and will unlock ideas. Begin to protect your ideas (intellectual property). Seek professional advice to help you with that.

Learn about the different levels of increase – 30, 60, 100, 1000 as well as the 4-fold, 7-fold increases and know-how and to what they apply.

Invest In People

Invest in people – gold, food, water and livestock – which are basic substances for man's survival.

For the economists and critics who don't believe God is real or still speaks – while praying, the Lord asked, "What if you had a major disaster – a war breaking out in the USA or an oil explosion in Russia, or a shaking on Wall Street, or riots in various nations or if a major earthquake hitting Italy? How would it affect countries like Jamaica and smaller/third world nations especially with the threat by the Trump Administration of tariffs to be levied on steel and aluminum?" I am sure countries would begin to distance themselves from the USA. The small business, and courier services in the USA and neighboring regions would feel the heat.

Tourism and immigration would also be negatively affected in the USA; and because many remit monies overseas from the USA, it will trigger a recession and suffering especially for smaller countries. Then we might see countries forfeiting on debt repayment and create another level of suffering. So we better start to renegotiate with the international lenders to restructure those loans before it is too late. Nations must have contingencies in place for these happenings.

A major appeal needs to be made to get everybody involved in farming and stockpile 10% of everything – whether it is bough or homegrown.

God created the economy before He created man. That being so, we need then to revisit and study God's prescribed order on how individuals and countries must operate, in order to have a solid economy. The further we pull away from the Kingdom Principles for governing, the more problems we will encounter. For example, foregoing a day of rest in order to grow the economy will not augur well for us, it will instead do more damage.

Also, implementing systems that would go against God's laws and precepts will affect the economy negatively.

Media houses need to reduce their advertising costs to small businesses and not for profit organizations and help them to grow in that area, and they will have loyal clients.

Farmers need donate 10% of their increase/harvest to the

- ✓ Poor and less fortunate
- ✓ Shelters, places of safety and even to feed the security forces of the nation,

and that will bring them (farmers) further increase in their yield.

The government needs to have dialogue with the people right away to chart a new economic direction as the old ways are dead.

Chapter 18

THE EAGLE MUST SOAR

As the United States of America prepares for the elections, there are may indications that regardless of whomever wins, there will be problems. America has been under attack from the Anti-Christ Spirit and the Spirit of Jezebel. The spiritual walls of the nation have broken down and the enemy has infiltrated – destroying families, the education system and the general fabric of the society. The media and Hollywood have also done significant damage. Witchcraft has also played a great role in doing damage to nation. In addition to this, over the years the enemy has divided the nation by many means including gender, sex and race.

The fact is that when you check the statistics anywhere, the United States of America is the top nation that gives most financially, particularly to Humanitarian work and Missions to advance the Kingdom of God. It is also the most vocal nation that speaks about and supports freedom of speech, freedom of expression and religion.

Over the years, however, the USA has allowed their spiritual gates and walls to be torn down, and as a result, Abortion, Gender Issues and Sexual Rights, the sexualization of Children and the ill-treatment of the poor to enter the nation. A nation that allows their future to be terminated (abortion) will struggle to have a future at all. Prophetically, there is now a fight for the "soul of the nation", as the United States has been leading the world and has great influence regarding the direction of the West.

In order for the eagle to soar, they must identify what made them great in the first place. They must also remain true to their motto – "In God We Trust". They must allow God to return to the Schools, the Community, the workplace and ensure that the grace of God is maintained and extended. They must begin to reach out again to poorer, smaller nations and help them. They must begin, like Nehemiah, to pray again and rebuild the gates; and it has to be the joint effort of all parties (political and otherwise). They cannot allow the enemy to continue to divide and destroy from within. They must identify the real enemy and deal with them as Nehemiah did.

The altar must be rebuilt for the revival to return to America. Leaders of every level must make atonement for the healing of the nation. They must understand that the poor of the nation are not the problem, but how they have mistreated and neglected the poor within. (Proverbs 31: 8 – 9)

The Church in America

The churches in the United States of America must necessarily return to the Great Commission, and begin to bring healing, restoration and reconciliation. They must remember that they are the salt and the light. They must be mutual politically. They should not get caught up in the devices of the enemy, like the issue of Race, the FOX

News and the CNN. They also need to understand spiritual warfare and how to rebuild the altar as Elijah did.

It was the eighteenth (18th)US President Ulysses S. Grant who spoke this word, "Hold fast to the Bible. To the influence of this Book we are indebted for all the progress made in true civilization and to this we must look as our guide in the future."

The thirtieth (30th) US President, President Calvin Coolidge said, "The strength of our country is the strength of its religious conviction. The foundation of our society and our government rests so much on the teaching of the Bible, that it would be difficult to support them if faith in this teaching would cease to be practically universal in our country."

The fourth (4th) President of the United States, President James Madison stated, "We have staked the whole future of American civilization not on the power of government, far from it. We have staked the whole of our political institutions upon the capacity of mankind for self-government, upon the capacity of each and all of us to govern ourselves according to the commandments of God. The future and success of America is not in this Constitution, but in the laws of God upon which this Constitution is founded."
It is the responsibility of every Christian globally to pray for the United States of America that they will fulfill their prophetic mandate and that the eagle will soar again.

Rededicate The Usa Flag

Covenants are very important, particularly covenants with God. God is revisiting all covenants with both individuals and nations.

Covenants and vows are what cause us to prosper and become great. When a covenant is broken, there are consequences – including turmoil and chaos.

Understand that a covenant comes with four (4) elements – parties, conditions, security and results. In the United States' Pledge of Allegiance, a covenant was made with God and that is why there is a fight. The Pledge of Allegiance includes the statement, "...*one nation, under God...*"

When covenants are made, it goes beyond the individual, group or nation making the covenant, it goes into lineage and connections.

A flag is not just a symbol, but a way for a country to portray itself to the rest of the world. Those who created the Flag of the United States used the colors and shapes they chose to embody what they felt the flag should symbolize. However, we must recognize that Prophetic symbols and colors are very important and carry powerful prophetic symbolism.

The enemy wants to remove everything that spiritually established the United States of America; and replace it with those things that glorify the devil instead. For example, the eagle symbolizes leader, prophet, a sharp/eagle-eyed view, sharp vision particularly from above. (Hosea 12: 13; Exodus 19: 4)

The Stars – symbolize that in the same way that the constellations in the night sky will stand "forever," the states of the nation and as a result, the nation itself, would stand forever. The stars on the flag represent the number of states in the union of states.

For them the Blue Star Field on which the stars sit represents justice and perseverance.

The Stripes – were incredibly symbolic in both color and number. The stripe design signified sun-rays shining down; a strong image when considering the birth of a new nation.

Red stripes were chosen to represent valor, courage and hardiness.

White stripes represented innocence and purity, a new country just born and starting on its own.

Even the number of stripes has meaning. Originally, the 13 stripes honor the original English colonies; those men and women who worked hard and sacrificed much to make it in the new world, the world becoming a new country. Today there are 50 stripes – 1 representing each state in the Union.

The Colors Of The USA Flag

White represents purity, holiness and redemption of sin. It also is also the official color of Church. It also represents victory over evil.

Blue is a heavenly color. Blue was used on the clothing of the priests and lined the hem of the priests' garments. (Exodus 28: 5 – 6). Blue was used in the tabernacle and the temple. It symbolizes heaven, the Holy Spirit and Truth. It also symbolizes healing.

The Flag Colors Prophetically

Red symbolizes the Blood of Jesus shed for us. It also denotes zeal and passion.

The problems that the USA I currently going through is about the fulfillment and purpose in the End Time. The focus should not be on racism. The focus should be rebuilding the walls and the gates that have been torn down.

It is the responsibility of each person to pray for the USA, particularly Christians, so that they will re-establish their covenant with God.

Rededicate the Nation

On June 24, 2020, the Lord gave me a word and said that the President of the United States will need to do a proclamation – a Day of Prayer and Re-dedication of the Flag to the Lord as a symbol of re-establishing the covenant with God. THIS IS URGENT!

Only then we will begin to see positive and significant change in the nation. The desecration and defilement will be broken. The division will be broken so that unity, and a united nation will emerge; humanity and compassion will increase and humanitarian efforts once again thrive.

Obeying such an instruction would bring change and be the beginning of peace. The nation must understand that it is fighting spiritual warfare. Division, Chaos and War are spirits. The enemy wants to abort the nation's purpose. So, it is key that the nation utilizes spiritual tools to deal with spiritual problems.

Homelessness In America

For some, the word **"home"** represents a place of comfort, unity, safety, stability; a place where your mind can be at ease and you feel loved – a place for family. But for many in our country and in our world today, they no longer have such a place. Now more than ever, there is a shortage of housing units that low-income people can afford. And as the gap between income and housing costs grows, more people face homelessness.

Revelations From The PIT

According to the 2018 HUD's **Point-In-Time (PIT)** report, (which is the only nation-wide survey of homeless people, provides this data and other useful statistics), approximately 552,830 people were experiencing homelessness in the United States on a single night. Homelessness has increased slightly by 0.3%, between 2017 and 2018 nationally. However, while the percentage is small, that represents 1,834 people – human beings without a place to live.

On a single night in 2018 there were approximately 3,976 people experiencing homelessness in Connecticut – 593 were evacuees from Puerto Rico after natural disasters. Furthermore, **67%** of people experiencing homelessness are **Individuals**. The remaining **33%** are people in **families with children**. **Youth** under the age of 25 and living on their own (without parents or children) account for **7%** of the homeless population; and **veterans** account for another **7%** of the total homeless population, and chronically homeless people. **Those with disabilities** who have been homeless for an extended period of time or repeatedly – comprise **18%** of the homeless population.

The homeless population is largely male. Among individual adults, 70 percent are men. Interestingly, White Americans are the largest racial grouping, accounting for **49%** of those experiencing homelessness. African Americans and American Indians **are dramatically overrepresented** in the **PIT** Count compared to their numbers in the general population.

Homeless individuals are experiencing far less progress, with their rates dropping by only 10%. The group broadly includes some subgroup members (Veterans, Chronically Homeless, Youth)—but most are adults who don't fall into any one of those categories. As the largest subgroup, making up **67%** of the total population, solutions for individuals are critical to efforts to end homelessness.

The State Of The States

State-level trends mirror those at the national-level. Thirty-eight (38) states have realized decreases in homelessness since 2007. Five states in particular top the list:

Michigan 70% (the largest percentage decrease); Kentucky 54%; Georgia 52%; West Virginia 48%; New Jersey 46%. On the opposite end of the spectrum, 12 states and the District of Columbia have experienced growths in homelessness that range from 1% in Iowa to 100 % in South Dakota.

Overall, the states with the greatest number tend to be the most populous. However, there are a few, including Oregon and Colorado, that top the homeless count list while having relatively smaller populations. 67% of people experiencing homelessness can be found in the ten states with the largest number of homeless people. New York, Hawaii, Oregon, California, and the District of Columbia top this list. These states and jurisdictions also have the highest housing costs in the country.

When it comes to healthcare, treatment and preventive care can be difficult to access for people who are homeless. This is usually because they lack insurance or have difficulty engaging health care providers in the community. Additionally, the homeless face significant obstacles to finding and maintaining employment. Finding a home is a critical first step. Job training and placement programs, such as those funded by the federal government, also provide the tools some people need to secure stable, long-term employment. Improving access to supportive services, such as childcare subsidies and transportation assistance, would also go a long way in helping people stay employed, achieve housing stability and remain housed.

The Global Scene

Globally, **Forced Displacement** is the major cause of homelessness – where people are forced to leave their home and oftentimes their country – usually because of war or civil injustices – in order to find a safer place to be. Today, according to the UNHCR – the United Nations Refugee Agency, Forced Displacement is at record 68.5 million. That means there are 68.5 million people who are homeless.

According to UNHCR reports published June 2019, "Wars, violence and persecution uprooted record numbers of men, women and children worldwide last year, making a new global deal on refugees more critical than ever..."

The number of asylum-seekers awaiting the outcome of their applications for refugee status had risen by about 300,000, to 3.1 million, by the end of December 2017. People displaced inside their own country accounted for 40 million of the 68.5 million - slightly fewer than the 40.3 million in 2016.

Homelessness, in all its forms, is real and it affects every region, nation, race, economy, community – everyone. Yet, while homelessness is a very serious problem, it also presents each one of us with the opportunity to reach out to those in need and allow the better part of our humanity to shine and bring true light where homelessness and hopelessness exist.

Chapter 19

THE WIND OF CHANGE AND VALUE OF LIFE

Many people want to have riches, fame and power, but they forget that the higher you go, the greater the problems and expectations will be. The key is to have God's help.

Everybody has problems - regardless of status. Having money/wealth doesn't mean there won't be problems. On the contrary, there will be problems, and some of the problems we will not be able to fix – only God can do that. This reminds us that we are not God and we do not have full control. Some may think that prayer doesn't work, but prayer brings supernatural intervention, not in the way we may expect, but in the way it is needed for real change to come.

Society is set up for people to fake it and pretend that everything is okay, and social network is the medium society has created to perpetuate the cover-up. I believe that the number one reason at the root of suicide is the inability of people to find God or someone with integrity that they can trust and be open with in order to get help to solve their problems. Trusting the wrong person will bring chaos and failure. Remember, your enemy is always the one who does not want to see the fulfilment of your purpose (it could be a family member, a friend - anyone)
I believe we are about to see the greatest shift on earth and part of the shift we are about to see is great men

and great organizations will just tumble in a day. Many will be shocked. But whosoever calls upon the name of the Lord will be saved. Find someone to trust! When problems arise remember, there is nothing more valuable than life and despite what you see there is ALWAYS hope! Things can change in a moment and anything you lose today you can get it back tomorrow. Remember the story of Job – he lost everything including his family; but God restored him and he received twice as much as he had before including family – because he stood through the situation. The main fact that you are still alive and God didn't take you out, means that you still have a fighting chance and you cannot give up. Material things are always temporary; they come in seasons and they can go in seasons. But when a person takes his/her own life, it is not a temporary thing, in fact, their real problem starts at that point and there is no rest in peace. Unlike this life, eternity does not end.

We all need to realize that problems are gates of change and they always test us for us to see what is really within us and in our hearts, and the strength and structure of our foundation. The question then becomes, "Of what material is our foundation/empire made?" (Matthew 7: 24 – 27)

Many build their foundation /empire trusting in man, their wealth, the size of their empire and even on their knowledge/wisdom, not remembering that all these will be tested. If the foundation/empire is not built on the Solid Rock, then the fall will be great.

Shift

The wind has shifted! When the wind shifts, it affects everything – authority, priority, as well as political and military direction and market conditions. If we – whether individually or collectively – don't shift with the shift then we will be shifted out and there will be great losses, not profits.

When the wind shifts, even an aircraft has to change direction in order to continue safely and avoid crashing. It is called "wind shear". In weather, a "wind shear" is a microscale meteorological phenomenon occurring over a very small distance. So we are in an unpredictable time where the seasons are irregular and so, where there was once predictability and comfortability those no longer exists. So many have plans – whether to go to war or gain power at any level – but only God's plan will be accomplished. As a result we now have to change the runway we use in order to safely get off the ground.

Things will become so serious, that even famous and historical landmarks will be utterly destroyed. So if people don't change the way they think and operate, we will see suicide rate will increase to a level we have never seen before.

Fake Society

Society is set up for people to fake it and pretend that everything is OK, and social network is the medium society has created to perpetuate the cover-up. I

248

believe that the number one reason at the root of suicide is the inability of people to find God or someone with integrity that they can trust and be open with in order to get help to solve their problems. Trusting the wrong person will bring chaos and failure. Remember, your enemy is always the one who does not want to see the fulfilment of your purpose (it could be a family member, a friend - anyone).

I believe we are about to see the greatest shift on earth, and part of the shift we are about to see is great men and great organizations will just tumbling in a day. Many will be shocked. But whosoever calls upon the name of the Lord will be saved. Find someone to trust! When problems arise, remember that there is nothing more valuable than life; and despite what you see, there is ALWAYS hope! Things can change in a moment and anything you lose today you can get it back tomorrow.

Churches will split and new church groups will rise up – new alliances, new political party, new prophets and those who we least expect will rise from seemingly nowhere to be used by God!

Stand And You Will See Change

Remember the story of Job - he lost everything, including his family; but God restored him and he received twice as much as he had before, including family - because he stood through the situation.

The main fact that you are still alive and God didn't take you out means that you still have a fighting chance and you should not give up. Material things are always temporary; they come in seasons and they can go in seasons. But when a person takes his/her own life, it is not a temporary thing; in fact, their real problem starts at that point and there is no resting in peace. Unlike this life, eternity does not end.

We all need to realize that problems are gates of change and they always test us to see what is really within us and in our hearts, and the strength and structure of our foundation. The question then becomes, "Of what material is our foundation/empire made?" (Matthew 7: 24-27)

Many build their foundation/empire trusting in man, their wealth, the size of their empire and even on their knowledge/wisdom, not remembering that all these will be tested. If the foundation/empire is not built on the Solid Rock, then the fall will be great.

The Heart Of The Good Samaritan (Luke 10: 25 - 37)

This is a Scripture that every leader, every Christian, every non-Christian needs to read if we truly want changes in the world, and if we truly want to stomp out anything that is contrary to God's Word. Some of us may say "We know the Law, we practice the Law" but are we doers of the Law. (Law here meaning the Word of God).

The Selfishness That Abounds

Notice that Jesus in response to the lawyer - who was supposed to be an expert in the Law, highlighted the Priest, and the Levite in His parable about the Good Samaritan; and showed that the Priest and the Levite passed the wounded man lying down on the side of the road - stripped and half dead. He was neglected. How many today are doing the same thing, yet we talk about racism, classism and are jumping on the racial injustice system bandwagon when there are different agendas. There are many that you pass daily without taking a second look. Selfishness abounds - that selfishness which is the commanding force of human nature. The Samaritans and the Jews were enemies, but this Samaritan's heart of compassion and mercy (which the world lacks) looked beyond the race, culture, color, and status and saw the person who needed help. We don't have a race problem, we have a heart problem, and our hearts are wicked - the heart that would pass someone who is hurting and in need.

Love Your Neighbor

Luke 10: 26 - 29 says, *"He said to him, "What is written in the law? What is your reading of it?" So he answered and said, " 'You shall love the Lord your God with all your heart, with all your soul, with all your strength, and with all your mind,' and 'your neighbor as yourself.' " And He said to him, "You have answered rightly; do this and you will live." But he, wanting to justify himself, said to Jesus, "And who is my neighbor?"*

We need to remember that our neighbor is not simply those of our own kind - our neighbor runs across racial, cultural, and color lines.

Why didn't the media highlight the years of neglect of the poor and voiceless by those in positions of authority and access to resources?

Change the World!

We must stop dividing the people and begin to help the people regardless of skin color.

Instead of continuing to allow Satan to divide us continually on issues of race, sex, and all these issues keeping us from seeing the truth and the real issues, seek the Lord for the Heart of the Good Samaritan and change the world!

Chapter 20

A TIME OF OUTPOURING

The COVID-19 Pandemic has exposed and shown the weaknesses of the local church. There has been very little taught regarding spiritual gifts and their purposes and that has contributed to the global crisis being experienced, and so there are very little solutions being brought forth, and this as deception increases.

There is a variety of spiritual gifts that have been afforded us. There are the Gifts of the Father, Gifts of the Son and Gifts of the Holy Spirit. In this article, I am focusing more on the Gifts of the Holy Spirit.

1 Corinthians 12: 7 says, *"But the manifestation of the Spirit is given to each one for the profit of all:"*

There many who ask from time to time – "What is my calling?" Others may ask, "What is my purpose or assignment?"

In my book, Know Your Calling In The Fivefold Ministry, answer some of the questions commonly asked. In my view, and based on my experience, I believe that over 70 per cent of Christians today have no clue as to their calling or purpose. It is a sad state of affairs, because not only is the Kingdom of God not benefitting, but the world is seeking for answers in the wrong places from the wrong sources – tarot cards, tea leaves, palm readers, psychic networks, obeah/mayal, and other occult activities. If members of the Body of Christ were utilizing their gits, then crime and violence would not be where it is today.

Sadly, the moment some Christians begin to manifest their gifts, they are persecuted and deemed evil by their peers. Also, theologists begin to manipulate then and tell them their gifts are not relevant to now. Some are even told that Apostles and Prophets no longer exist only Pastors, Evangelists. As a result, there are many churches which are without the head, eyes or brain! It is interesting that the word Apostle is mentioned 83 times; Prophets 172 times and Pastors only 1 time.

Ephesians 2: 20, states that they are the foundation for the Church. So, why do they want to undo what God has established? So, if there are no Apostles and Prophets in the Church, why would there be Pastors?

Thus, the revival that God wants to do and that the Church needs is being hindered and it is the same members of the Body of Christ which are in fact hindered. So, the local churches are now headless, and that stops them from effectively dealing with the spiritual warfare, and the deception coming from every wind of doctrine, including the utterances of scientists that have been given precedence in the House of God/Body of Christ, over the instructions and guidance of the Holy Spirit.
It is important to note that among the deceptions, is untruth that not everybody can have access to the giftings of the Holy Spirit as recorded in 1 Corinthians 12, and they make particular mention of, speaking in tongues; which we must realize is a grace given to every

individual. (1 Corinthians 14) It is our personal protocol language to communicate directly to God in heaven. This allows us to pray accurately according to the will of God for our lives, nation and church, and deal with Spiritual Warfare effectively to unlock the mysteries of God and bring solutions in the earth. (Romans 8; Matthew 7: 11, Luke 11: 13)

Speaking in tongues is different from the gifts of Diverse Tongues and Interpretation of Tongues. Please note that the gifts of Diverse Tongues and the Interpretation of Tongues are each part of the 9 gifts of the Holy Spirit. (1 Corinthians 12; Joel 2: 28; Acts 1: 8, Acts 2: 1 – 4). Speaking in tongues is not among those 9 gifts. Again, it is a grace given to all so they may be effectively edified. By virtue of 1 Corinthians 14, it would mean that many today are not being edified, and that needs to change. So, let it be clear, that a person can be baptized by the Holy Spirit evidenced by them speaking in tongues, but, that does not mean they possess the gift of Diverse Tongues nor the Interpretation of Tongues.

That being said, we should not confuse what Paul the Apostle said in 1 Corinthians 14 regarding private self-edification with tongues in a corporate gathering. In part 2, I will go on further in explaining the gifts of the Holy Spirit.

The Gifts Of The Holy Spirit Explained

The 9 Gifts of the Holy is divided into 3 groups that I call Illuminative Gifts, Oral Gifts and Dominative Gifts. There are diversities of gifts but the same spirit. There are differences of ministries but the same Lord. (1 Corinthians 12: 4 – 5)

The number 9 is significant and symbolizes divine completeness or conveys the meaning of finality. Christ died at the 9th hour of the day. It also represents the fruit of God's Holy Spirit – so the 9 gifts and the 9 fruits work together to get a harvest. (Galatians 5: 22 – 23)

A person can have the gifts, but don't possess the fruit of the spirit and as such will not reap the necessary harvest they should. Prayer which bring harvest to the Body of Christ.

The number 9 shows up many times in the Scriptures. For example, Peter went to the Temple in the 9th hour, Cornelius fasted until the 9th hour and so we see that the number 9 has to do with intercession. Intercession using the gifts would do wonders.

The Gifts

Word of Wisdom

The first gift recorded was the Word of Wisdom which is a Spiritual gift given which supernaturally discloses the mind, purpose and will of God as applied for specific situations. It also gives you insight and foresight for what lies ahead. For example, Joseph in the Bible utilized this gift mightily in order to come up with a plan for the famine ahead. Wisdom also reveals the best way that knowledge should be used. This gift is also good for judges, security personnel, and other leaders including Presidents and Prime Ministers.

Word of Knowledge

Knowledge which supernaturally reveals the past and present situation pertaining to a person or an event. For example, a person may stand before you and the Lord may reveal very important information regarding their past and present. This gift is very helpful in solving crime and violence or other health issues and other security issues.

Gift of Faith

The gift of Faith supernaturally goes beyond ordinary faith – whether it is saving faith. It means that someone with this gift trusts God without a doubt. They can also discern with extraordinary confidence. We need that gift now to deal with crisis and the pandemic.

The Gift of Healing

We all have the ability to lay hands on the sick and they recover. However, the person with the Gift of Healing supernaturally has the ability to deal with many sicknesses, diseases and disorder. They may have 100% accuracy in bringing restoration and healing to those who are sick.

Gift of Working of Miracles

The Working of Miracles is a manifestation of God's powers beyond the ordinary course of natural laws. This gift will do what the natural man cannot do naturally. We need this gift in times of emergency and when things become impossible.

Gift of Prophecy

This is a divine gift that supernaturally reveals the future. It brings edification, revelation, insight and comfort. This gift is needed more than ever to prevent disaster, direction and much more.

Discerning of Spirits

This is the ability to discern which spirit is in operation – good or bad? It discerns demonic, satanic, false, fake and detects the true source of circumstances and motives, lies and deceivers. This is needed more than ever in this time of deception.

Diverse Tongues

This deals with speaking in and understanding different languages without having studied/learned them. So, God will give us many languages in order to receive and communicate a message from God to His people.

Interpretation of Tongues

Interpreting the meaning of different tongues declared within a public setting or corporate gathering, that the people may know the message spoken to the gathering in the unknown tongues, for the edifying of those within that setting.

So, it is critical for every member to seek for these gifts and utilize them in the end time, which will bring revival, save lives and bring necessary change for the benefit of all.

Chapter 21

GLOBAL LEADERS NEED TO CHANGE THEIR FOCUS

For many years we have been telling global leaders to change their focus and that the direction they are going is not beneficial to the nations. Their focus has been economic and social development – the issues such as gender, sexual rights and other issues that are not relevant to human development. We have seen more people getting poorer, people being marginalized, people ignoring the cries of the poor; people are ignoring the environmental clues and signs and continue to build in areas that should be utilized for charting river courses and for farming. The globe has developed a culture of greed where most leaders no longer planning for the future, nor are the making preparations for the next generation. So, unless there is a global shift, we are heading for a humanitarian crisis.

The United Nations

The United Nations and all its bodies need to change the way they operate. Most member states will simply give reports on paper to look good, but the real issues that take place on the ground are not being highlighted. It is critical that they begin trying new things, such as finding 20 people from the general public – homeless included – to speak before the chairman and other representatives.

There are many speaking on Sustainable Development, but they are guilty of ignoring the poor. Many of the needs of the poor are being ignored. Most don't have food to eat, and we are seeing nations cutting welfare and other benefits. They have not food to eat or clothes to wear.

Get Back To The Core Focus

The core focus should be restoration. Instead of the multiple, pricey retreats for self, use some of that money and get food for those in need to eat, clothes to wear and put them up in inexpensive but clean hotels so they can bathe, brush their teeth and feel human again.

God Displeased With Global Leaders

We are in a time where many are experiencing great disappointment, and some feel deep betrayal, with the leaders of their nations. Many don't know who to trust, politically and they don't see much differences in the philosophies being presented to them as plans for their nation.The poor have been forgotten and forsaken.

We are seeing history repeating itself, and we are now seeing the days of Amos return. Amos stressed that righteousness and justice are essential for a healthy society. During that time, ancient Israel enjoyed great prosperity. They gained control of international trade routes and the kings' highways through Transjordan. They restored borders and great expansion and economic development. The nation reached new political and military heights, but the religious situation was at an all time low. Idolatry was rampant and the rich were living in luxury while the poor were oppressed. There was widespread immorality and the judicial system was corrupt. At that time, the people interpreted the prosperity they saw as a sign of God's blessing. But God was displeased with the nations and He said, unless there was a change of heart – a change that would allow "justice to run down like water and righteousness like a mighty stream". Then all nations would experience famine. It would be a famine not for food but a famine for the Word of God.

Famine For The Word

A famine is a widespread scarcity of food caused by several factors, including war, inflation, crop failure, population imbalance or government policy. (Amos 8: 11 - 12) When there is a famine of the Word of God, it will affect everything. It brings judgement, lack of truth, deception, strong delusions; evil will increase which will bring death, debt, confusion, environmental problems, lack of direction, lack of wisdom, confusion, riots, broken families and refugee crises. Many churches will be empty. People will be travelling from all over the world trying to find the truth.

Famine and drought were two of the punishments God used against ancient Israel. Amos speaks of a new kind of famine -the lack of the Word of God. No assurance would be available that God will hear their cries for help;

and no direction from God will guide them in their time of need. All will be silent.

All nations under God's control must and will answer to Him for the treatment of other nations and peoples. Social injustices, the wasted extravagance, corporate greed and social inequality are evident today as it was then. 20% of the world consumes 80% of the world's goods. We are seeing human rights being violated without conscience. The same poor that vote for political leaders are now being trampled.

Leaders vs. Rulers

There is a difference between Leaders and Rulers. God is looking for leaders who will open their mouths for the voiceless, the homeless who will plead the cause for the poor the needy, the voiceless and those who suffer great injustices.

Many politicians now see the poor as a burden and are being treated that way. After they are elected the mete out harsh treatment to the people.

Every leader needs to know that they are servants, not owners or masters, and that they are employed by the people; and that it is the same God that gives the leaders favor, and who control the further and destiny of that leader. The people also, in order to receive good leadership must return to God.

There are many seeking political office, but the question to those who do should be, "Why am I seeking political office? Am I doing it for the betterment of the poor or is it for the investors, or is it for a personal agenda?" The truth is, time will tell.

Unless there is a heart change, then the five (5) symbolic visions outlined in the Scriptures will manifest – Locust, Fire, the Plumb Line, the Basket of Fruits and God beside the Altar. (Amos 7 & Amos 9)

There is hope. The Book of Amos tells us that restoration will take place. So, we pray for restoration, rebuilding and repair and changes in the heart that will take place, so that we may receive the environmental change we need.

Chapter 22

GOD STILL SPEAKS – SIGNS OF TIMES

Luke 21: 25 says, "And there will be signs in the sun, in the moon, and in the stars; and on the earth distress of nations, with perplexity, the sea and the waves roaring;"

We are seeing these six (6) occurrences taking place in the earth like never before.

Over the years we have been prophesying about these things and in the Word of the Lord for 2018 (Part 3) these things were also prophesied. Read number 2, 7, 15, 16, 17, 19, 33 and 34.

We have seen the devastation caused by fires, in different parts of the United States – California, the Carolina as well as volcanic eruptions in Hawaii and other parts of the world; as well as earthquakes in Indonesia with death toll of 300 and rising. There is even a major disaster in Florida as was prophesied – they call it the red tide; Dolphins, sharks and other marine life are perishing in alarming numbers and are being washed up on the shores. Scientists say the worst is to come. All this is having a negative impact on marine life as well as human consumption and economic growth. The questions we need to ask are, "Is the consumption of fish still safe?", "Is our water system still safe for human consumption?" "Is there addition testing to ensure that there is no further disease breakout?" and "How safe and stable is our communication system, are we ready for a blackout"

While many talk about global warming, the greatest hindrance to the environment are human beings. Our own actions have been destroying our environment. Weapons testing and polluting the ocean for economic gain. Scientists also have gone beyond their human boundaries and some of what they are doing is impacting negatively on the environment. We are now seeing an increase in "freak" occurrences such as freak storms and flash floods.

In Genoa, Italy August 14, 2018, strong winds caused a raised highway to collapse killing at least 25 and injuring 11 pulled from the rubble – according to Genoa's Mayor Marco Bucci.

Further to that, on August 8, 2018, a rare fire tornado was reported in the United Kingdom appropriately referred to it as a "firenado." Firefighters in Derbyshire, England, captured a strange and frightening natural phenomenon on video Tuesday.

God Still Speaks

God has been speaking from the time of creation until today. He speaks through His servants and when man refuses to listen to God's servants, then man pays the price. We have been destroying the planet for the sake of greed – greedy organizations who influence nations and politicians to pass unjust laws which impact and affect us all particularly the poor the fatherless and the voiceless within a nation.

The number one threat to the planet is not global warming or climate change it is sin, because sin affects the climate (read the Book of Genesis) and the very animals are now being impacted/affect and this will affect human beings consuming them as food.

Scientists will now become bankrupt of ideas and answers because they no longer acknowledge Him as the Creator. Many are now worshipping the creation without realizing that the very creation depends on God for sustenance and relevance of purpose (Psalms 148)

It is critical for different leaders and lawmakers to come together to develop a plan which could be driven by the United Nations to help save lives and deal with other disasters which could be coming.

Several prophecies in Part 3 of the Word of the Lord 2018 published in the Gleaner (Jamaica)

#2 Focus on Revelation 5, Revelation 8, and Revelation 18. We are going to see a lot of problems with the cosmos (cosmic convulsions) similar to Exodus 10: 21 – as a sign of God's displeasure in the earth. There will be a lot of activity on/with the sun, and scientists will have their hands full. There will be problems with vegetation as well as volcanic eruptions, increase of earthquakes in diverse places, and serious problems with marine life. May fish will die and there will be great pollution. Meteors will fall and there will be increased testing of weapons in the sea. (Joel 2: 30 – 32, Jeremiah 9: 15 – 23). All these things will affect crop, property, and life. We will be seeing greater flooding, more bloodshed, and pestilence.

#7 There will be wars in the ocean. Many problems will arise in the oceans, which can cause major losses, especially with tuna fish. Many who eat tuna fish will get sick because of ocean contamination.

#16 Nations need to be ready to assist other nations because a chemical disaster is at large. Many seas are going to be polluted due to rebellion in man throughout the ecosystem. I saw in the Spirit the extinction of Dolphins due to severe pollution. Due to the severe pollution that will be taking place, many will become infected from every class level. However, the poor will be more susceptible to the health hazards.

#19 Fires will burn in diverse places in America, Africa, and west of Indonesia.

#26 We will see cyber-electronic devices, IDs, and other data-driven systems that will be implemented under the guise of boosting national security and bringing economic growth to countries, but the Lord tells His people to be ready.

Healing By Miracle Or Medicine

No one wants to be sick, yet today there are many – millions who are sick today and their category, color, race or social standing was not the deciding factor.

The Holy Spirit wants to heal, but before the healing takes place the mind has to be at the place of embracing the Healer, the healing and the method. God can use or allow medicine, nutrition or miracles to do so and He can and will often do it in unorthodox ways; ways that defy and challenge logic. Sadly, there are many who die, because they refuse to change their mindset about healing – even Christian leaders who are supposed to believe in the power of God.

We will want to discredit God's power while ignoring several scriptures in the Bible. (Matthew 16: 17 – 18). Interestingly, the major part of Jesus' ministry dealt with healing and that was why He became famous.

Every sickness has a root and that root is spiritual. Infirmity is a spirit (or a curse) and there are many diseases and illnesses that fall under that umbrella of infirmity. There may be lack of certain things within the body which may cause a sickness. In the Bible God uses different methods to bring healing to different ones including medicine – herbs and natural extracts. He also used doctors and His servants with the gift of healing to heal different people. (1 Corinthians 12: 9; 2 Kings 20: 1 – 11; Isaiah 38: 1 – 8) In the same way we go to the doctor and he checks into our family's medical history. There are many sicknesses that may come down through the lineage based on the sins committed by our fore-parents – including sexual sins, witchcraft or injustice. That is why it is key for Christian medical doctors who understand this to rise up. You cannot medicate a spiritual problem, nor can you give complete help if all areas are not addressed.

Many may say, "He is not a doctor, he can't talk about healing!" But that is the problem in the world today. Interestingly, Isaiah the Prophet did not study medicine, he studied what we would call International Relations. When the king Hezekiah was about to die from his illness, the king began to pray and seek God refusing to accept the fate of death. The prophet directed the king to apply poultice of figs which many medical scholars today say is an antibiotic. We also see again in 2 Kings 5: 1 – 15, a mighty and great commander who had leprosy. Leprosy today is known as Hansen's disease which is a long-lasting infection caused by bacteria which affects the skin, eyes and nervous system. Hansen's disease is treated with a combination of antibiotics. Typically, 2 or 3 antibiotics are used at the same time. In the Bible, God gave His prophet an instruction/prescription for this great commander – to go and dip seven times in the muddy Jordan River. What would the medical scholars and intellectuals of today say about that in response? Maybe they would say that the prophet of God had a psychotic disorder and needs Zyprexa, Rexulti or maybe even some Abilify. Others who would receive that instruction – based on their status (and level of pride) would probably think it a foolish instruction, walk away and find a way to fly out for treatment, since they don't even have confidence in their local health system. Naaman himself thought it was nonsense when the maid told him the instruction from the prophet of God. Nevertheless, he obeyed the instruction. Sometimes the place the Lord is sending you has exactly what you need for your healing even if you don't see or understand it. What if the state of the muddy river had the bacteria necessary to fight the bacteria affecting his skin and body?

Following Divine instructions and having an open mind to the things of God is the key for your healing. You may be directed to go on a 3-day Fast for God to give you instructions or you may be instructed to go and show yourself to the priest (Luke 17: 12 – 14) who will anoint you with oil and pray for your recovery.

Something as simple as Forgiveness or taking communion, being anointed with oil by God's anointed servant, changing your diet and an understanding of herbs and their uses can bring healing.

There are many within the society today suffering from various illnesses – some are even afraid to confide in family members. The question is, what are you willing to do to be healed?

Chapter 23

LACK OF MORAL VALUES DESTROYING NATIONS

Growing up, there were certain morals, standards and ethical guidelines that we were taught to follow. Most of our values were taken from the Bible and they served us well. Children were disciplined and the levels of crime and violence were not as high as they are today. We have allowed different people in different capacities to influence our standards and morals. The respect students held for their teachers, the esteem in which people held their leaders in society including pastors and those in public, private and civil society are almost non-existent today. The word today is that people have "evolved" from the way that is right.

Political Correctness

One of the biggest problems we have in society today is political correctness. Everyone wants to be popular – to the detriment of our nation. A true leader does what is right regardless of any political fallout because they would have the backing of God. Today, many make decisions to please others. There was a time that uncovering a person's nakedness in public and in the workplace would be a disgrace. Now, both men and women are leaving very little to the imagination – wearing very little with almost everything being exposed. They have become a stumbling block for others, yet there are many crying out about sexual harassment. No one wants to look at the core of the issue and deal with it.

Everything Goes, Anything Goes

In order to please the small percentage of people within society – who are sadly those with the money that makes the mare run – we are removing the moral guidelines and erasing the lines of demarcation regarding our principles we are promoting flagrant use of expletives and other un-Godly things as solutions to our society's ills. When everything goes, then anything goes and we should not then be surprised. When we see what is taking place in our schools, we need to stop blaming teachers. If we don't restore positive moral values to
our nation, soon every teacher may have to arm him/herself in order to survive in the school system.

Our ministry of Education and our Parent Teachers' Associations need to stand up, otherwise our schools will become garrisons and go-go clubs. Students should not be allowed to use cell phones at school unless there is an emergency and they are given permission. Many seem to prefer having the students arrested rather then being disciplined and set on the right track early in life. Very shortly we are going to hear that children have a right not to go to school or they should be allowed to go to school in pajamas. Maybe, they will say that they should be allowed to smoke marijuana because they feel it enlightens the mind. Maybe they will say it is okay to get pregnant and have multiple abortions or that they have the right to kill whoever they feel like killing. So, here are my questions. What about the rights of the parents? Are the parents recognizing what is happening?

Politicians And Morals

The number one criterion for being a representative of the people, should not be popularity, money, education, whether or not they have a Benz or a yacht. Morals, values and proper attitudes must be the criteria.

Morals are the principles we follow that help us to know the difference between right and wrong. So, when immoral people get power, they will advocate for immoral acts and laws. There are many who act honorable by day and are the complete opposite at night.

We have seen morals breakdown in media, politics, the marketplace and the church. A quick look at the advertisements and their messages reveal much, and when our young people respond accordingly, then there is an outcry against our youth, rather than the catalyst for their behavior.

When there are churches celebrating Halloween, having Bingo and have magicians and hypnotists coming in to entertain their congregation, when the church is supposed to be set apart and living in holiness, something is wrong. Righteousness, truth, grace, mercy, respect, honor, loyalty and Biblical principles build a nation to be strong. Moral values are of such that they should guide our bilateral agreements and deal making. Realize that when morals and values breakdown, it impacts climate change.

Leaders Should Learn From Jesus

As we celebrate this Christmas season, it is time for us to reflect on why Jesus came. It is unproductive to get into arguments about whether He was born in December or not; and it is imperative for us to celebrate Him by doing the things He taught us.

Jesus Christ came to redeem mankind and is mankind's only hope. Isaiah 9: 67 tells us about His names and His attributes. A Child Who was born to reign forever upon the throne of David; a Wonderful Counselor. He is an exemplary political guide and a leader, the Living Word and the infallible source of guidance. He is Inexhaustible Wisdom, the Truth and the Way, and on Him rests the governments. He is the True Hero of His people. Which god do you know that died for His people to set them free from bondage? He is a Divine Warrior, and the only One Wo can bring peace in the earth. Jesus demoted Himself to promote us and allow us to become rich. (Psalm 66)

What Is The Focus

Jesus never focused on self or on earthly power. All those are temporary. He taught us to seek the kingdom first and that all things would be added thereafter. Jesus wasn't born into a wealthy family although He owned the

275

World and created everything. He taught us that material things are not all there is to focus on in life. He taught us that there is immeasurable value in human beings. He wasn't born in a hospital, or 5-star hotel, neither did He have health insurance – "Obamacare", "Trumpcare", nor "Holnesscare". He was a champion or the poor because He identified with the poor.

Jesus showed us that where you were born, the family into which you were born or your status, does not determine your future and have nothing to do with achieving greatness. One Who was seen only as a carpenter's son, Who was despised by the academic community and the rabbis of the day because of where He was born, much like it is today in the way we treat those from the inner-city. He didn't graduate from the Harvards and from the Ivy League Universities of the day, yet He confounded and amazed them with His wisdom and knowledge. He taught the two (2) most important principles of leadership – humility and servanthood; reminding us all that when we enter into leadership at any level, we are called to serve, not to be served. He is a True Servant-Leader and Transformer of lives. He didn't have four (4) jets and innumerable security personnel, and His number one priority was upgrade the lives of the poor. Jesus never carried out His function to please the people, He did everything He did to please His Father. HE did not make decisions for the sake of popularity. He never turned the poor away – He fed them spiritually and physically. Even more so, He did not practice to be politically correct in His communication. Everything He did, He prayed to His Father.

Advice

He didn't seek the advice of other businessmen, Prime Ministers, and Nation Leaders, to implement their plans on His people. He sought the Father for solutions. And ever when there was great need among them, He practiced one of the greatest economic solutions. (Luke 9: 10 – 17) He looked up to God the Father, He blessed, then broke it then gave the resources to be distributed among the people; He knew that without His Father's blessings it would be useless to try and manage an economy and distribute the resources. Furthermore, He picked up the fragments, because He understood that there was money in the fragments – solidifying the principle that everything and everyone, including the rejected (fragments) have value and can be used. So, Jesus would never ever have a Christmas party, for example, and only invite who He believed was in His category or supported His agenda.

Jesus showed us two very important lessons – the Power of Prayer and the importance of the Holy Spirit in our daily roles and functions.

In addition to that, Jesus was willing to go where no one else was willing to go and He understood (and still does) the importance of Timing and Preparation. He went were the needs were.

Let us learn from Jesus.

Nation Needs Emotional Healing

We are living in a society that is broken and needs healing. There are many in influential positions within the society that need emotional healing but it cannot be done through/by medical resources, only through Spiritual empowerment and deliverance.

A person who needs spiritual and emotional healing first has to identify the root cause. Then the process starts with forgiveness, which is key. Many who have suffered emotionally have experienced that suffering through painful circumstances such as rape, absence of parent(s), and verbal/physical abuse in childhood by family members or others; it could even be as a result of negative words spoken by a teacher or schoolmate.

There are many who have been told that they would never amount to anything good. Interestingly, because of this kind of abuse, many persons take on different levels of academic study to prove their naysayers wrong. Some, as a result, become professional students accumulating degree upon degree.

If a person is motivated to achieve success based on negative circumstances, they are still not yet healed from the root issue. Many have chosen careers that God did not intend for them. People who have not yet experienced joy, despite their success can only receive the level of emotional healing they need through the Holy Spirit. Some will go into many forms of spiritualism in their pursuit for healing and joy - yoga, transcendental meditation and so on, but they will not find the true joy there – it simply creates a cycle of mood swings, instability and leaves them unable to maintain relationships while blaming others. Some become cold and even abusive at the workplace.

Being Whole

The people of a nation cannot enjoy true prosperity until they are emotionally healed and are whole – body, mind, soul, and spirit. (3 John 2) Why do you believe some people try hard drugs, and alcohol, engage in promiscuous, reckless sexual activities or even become gamblers or workaholics? They know that something is wrong, but all they are doing is so that they can experience peace.

There are those who, because of the love they did not experience growing up, they try to pour out that love upon their own children, but to the point of yielding to their every request and "spoiling" them – which is just as damaging. So they are more of a friend to their children than they are a parent and this creates a different problem. So as a result of that, those children are on a path to classism, pride/arrogance and even crime.

Emotional problems are worse than physical problems, because emotional problems cannot be addressed as readily since they are intangible.

Emotional problems influence our choices and behavior and affects the nation more than we think. Some of these problems are also linked to what takes place with the mother during pregnancy. Contrary to some beliefs, life begins at conception. The mother's environment and what the experience emotionally affects them and the child/children they carry. For example if they smoke or drink or are living in an environment where violence takes place regularly, then it is quite likely that the children they carry will do similarly. Recognize that our very calling and purpose are decided in the womb (Jeremiah 1: 5; Isaiah 49: 1; Luke 1: 39 – 45). Children who also survive attempted abortions grow up with a lot of emotional problems.

God's Presence Heals

The main reason God gives us gifts of healing, word of knowledge, and word of wisdom and discernment is to help to administer emotional healing (Luke 5: 17). God wants us to be emotionally stable so that there is overall stability. A simple environment with songs of worship even within the workplace can bring emotional healing. Some may feel peace and have goose pimples – like a distressed Saul did when David played. (I Samuel 16: 23). It brings refreshing and inner healing. Many would have diagnosed Saul's problem as a mental problem and medicate/sedate him. But his problem was emotional and spiritual.

We need to stop looking at the "quietness" of an individual as being a mark of emotional stability. A person can be quiet on the surface but have a myriad of emotions swirling within waiting for the button to be pushed.

Divine prosperity is not a momentary phenomenon, it is an on-going, progressing state of success and well-being. It is intended for every area of one's life spiritually, physically, emotionally and materially.

For us to move from poverty to prosperity, we can only achieve that (and deal with the crime issue) when we begin to deal with the emotional healing needed, especially by those in influential positions in every sector of our society.

God-Approved Vs. Man-Appointed

The recent elections in the United States of America has opened global discussions again, especially among Christians about a God-approved leader versus a man-appointed leader.

It is critical for the five-fold ministry to properly empower the people within the nations about the results and consequences of their choices. Further to this, if a person does not know God's way, how will they come to the knowledge of His will? The biggest fight we go through is the fight to know God's will and purpose. So many don't know the purpose for their own lives, so wrong choices are made and detrimental consequences result.

For anyone seeking political leadership, or in fact leadership of any kind, know that there are always conditions attached to your decision-making. (Deuteronomy 28). So, in order to maintain God's favor and grace, a leader has to know that the purpose for their coming into power is to accomplish God's will and His purpose, particularly regarding the care of the poor, the fatherless and the widow. It is never about a leader's mandates and motives – it is always about God. A nation always receives leadership based on their relationship with God. If the nation is good and has a heart for God and His will, then they will get a leader according to that state of heart.

The heart of a leader is also key to the selection and approval of the leader by God. Oftentimes, we select leaders based on external factors only – speech, color, gender – but God looks at the heart, according to 1 Samuel 16: 7, which says, "But the Lord said to Samuel, "Do not look at his appearance or at his physical stature, because I have refused him. For the Lord does not see as man sees; for man looks at the outward appearance, but the Lord looks at the heart."

Know that no leader is indispensable. If a leader does not follow the instructions or principles of God, then God will shift him/her out, and it is key that every religious advisor advises based on the Biblical truth and not personal opinion for gain nor fame.

God-Approved Leaders

God-Approved leaders carry His grace, His blessing, His favor, Peace, His Wisdom, Victory and Prosperity, and promote righteousness. Right things begin to happen. The right door opens, healing will take place and protection will be assured for the nation, when they have the God-approved Leaders.

Man-Approved Leaders

Man-approved leaders result in wars from within, poverty, sinful agenda, unrighteous laws, death, terrorism, lack of growth within the economy, population control, conspiracy, treason, corruption, defeat at the hands of the enemy, chaos and confusion. So when leaders God did not appoint, rise to power, it is an indication of the people rejecting God. When we reject God's rulership over us and our nation, then we have automatically accepted the devil's rulership.

In 1 Samuel 8, God clearly outlines the consequences that result when the people make wrong choices for leadership, and everyone should read that scripture. It further speaks of taxation, lack of mercy on the poor, and how that will cause the people to be engulfed in bondage. Deuteronomy 17: 14 - 20 further outlines to us the dos and the don'ts of leadership selection within a nation -including the fact that leaders must not multiply their own horses and must instead look to God. All trust and hope must be in God.

For example, a God-approved leader would consult God first in how to deal with the pandemic and other issues affecting the nation. A man appointed leader would put their trust in man, and Jeremiah 17: 5 – 9 clearly outlines the results of both decisions.

A God-approved leader's trust is in God to direct in times of war. A man-appointed leader's trust is in the nation's army, man-made devices, and weaponry.

The People

It is critical for the people to repent and return to God, if they truly want change. We must also remember that regardless of which leader reigns, God still remains King and our Savior. God can accomplish His will through any leader. Look at Nebuchadnezzar. Knowing God's will for our lives is first and foremost. Any woman will tell you that while we may have some level of success, making the wrong choices always brings pain.

Chapter 24

POVERTY AND CLIMATE CHANGE

Over twenty (20) years ago, world leaders in assessing the global landscape, agreed on the Millennium Development Goals (MDGs): a set of time-bound and quantified targets for addressing the many dimensions of extreme poverty, including hunger, disease, lack of adequate shelter, and exclusion; while promoting gender equality, education, and environmental sustainability. When the MDGs were agreed, there was a general acknowledgement of the fact that social development is a key component of the sustainable development of the whole human race. It works in tandem with economic, political and other forms of development.

Regrettably, in the intervening years, uneven and unequal global development meant that although some progress was made, many countries, particularly developing ones, failed to meet some of the MDGs. Today, more than 1 billion people still live in extreme poverty. They continue to struggle with limited access to basic services, including education, health services, safe drinking water and sanitation. Rising inequality and exclusion, unemployment and lack of decent work opportunities also remain problems in many countries. These unattained, social dimensions of development comprise much of the "unfinished business" of the MDGs that led to the calls for a new global paradigm to succeed them.

Today, there are more national disasters happening globally, and as I have said in previous articles, poverty and climate change and the new wave of natural disasters occurring are urgent issues on which we need to focus and act.

Most countries don't remember the agreement they made when they all came together in 2000. They are no longer living up to their promises and responsibilities. The drastic measures now being put in place – cutting benefits to the people, implementing stringent laws and practices that hurt rather than help are now negatively affecting the peoples of the nations to the detriment of their country.

For example, the 2017 Hurricane Season is the most costly in history racking up damages totaling US$370 billion worldwide, with over US$200 billion in damages occurring in the United States of America. The question is, if the natural disasters continue their current trend, and even affect those areas where oil is being drilled, for example, then how will we all be affected? Will oil prices skyrocket? Will we be able to afford petrol? How will that affect public transportation costs?

As things stand, over 783 million people are living below the international poverty line of US$1.90 per day. How will a continuation of these disasters affect that situation? What contingency plans do governments globally have for these occurrences?
3 out of every 10 persons lack access to safely managed drinking water and 6 out of every 10 people lack access

to safely managed sanitation facilities. Should the disasters continue, how do they impact this situation?

Solutions and Priority Shifts

We have a crisis and Governments, Businesses and Civil Society now must come together and change their focus. They must begin to focus more on the poor. Many talk about cyber security and this digital era, meanwhile people are not just suffering but are dying as a result of neglect. Cyber, digital and all that will mean nothing when someone is sick and hungry.

Nations need to actively engage in intensive food security programs at both national and individual levels. This extends to protecting marine life, including fish stocks which, given environmental and other threats to the oceans, means the world food supply will diminish even further as world population grows and more natural disasters take place.

Give more support for farming, not only in promoting it as a viable means of income Farming – those in poverty-stricken nations have a low-scale farming. So training is needed for them to improve their farming methods and output. Thus productivity will increase and a market can be established for the produce.

Support the development of micro-industries such as plant nurseries to grow flowers; or water purification plants to produce water for sale, thereby creating employment.

Make warehouse space available for storage of basic items.

Remove tax and customs duties from food items, water, tents and certain basic medical equipment and farmers' tools.

Governments must work with NGOs and Churches to coordinate plans for assistance. There also needs to be more training on issue fueling poverty as well as a harnessing of ideas from the people of the nation.

Climate Change And God

"You alone are the Lord; You have made heaven, the heaven of heavens, with all their host, The earth and everything on it, the seas and all that is in them, And You preserve them all. The host of heaven worships You." (Nehemiah 9: 6)

As we read this Scripture, we (as well as the 150 countries that gathered in the Paris recently) must realize that there can be no debate or discussion on climate change without including God.

The meetings were held in an effort to come up with a workable plan to stave off global catastrophe ahead. When we change – when mankind chooses to change their way of thinking and of operating, then we will not have to worry about climate change.

Before the fall of man, the original order of man's environment on earth must be distinguished from what it became following the impact of man's fall. The curse and the eventual deluge; the agricultural. the zoological, geological and meteorological dis-harmony to which creation has become subject must not be attributed to God! God gave us a perfect earth. It is man's sin that has brought about what man refers to as climate change.

Global leaders who want to have a serious discussion and solutions about climate change, must have the Bible as a guide going all the way back to Genesis and see how man's actions affect the globe.

Climate change does not only affect mankind. It affects the earth, the environment, the animals and the sea also. The rebellion of man against God and the push to have a Godless society is a greater threat than climate change.

Man's rebellion in times past brought about a great flood. It also caused a permanent change in weather activity called rain. Prior to rain, there was only mist and dew. Furthermore, the appearance of the rainbow is a symbol that God will not destroy the entire earth again by flood. (Genesis 9: 11 – 13; Genesis 8: 22)

The Solution To Climate Change Is Jesus!

Isaiah 24: 5 – 6 clearly outlines what things can defile the earth and cause climate change. It speaks about violating spiritual laws which can bring defilement within the earth – including rebellion against God, war, injustice, breaking God's covenant, negative speech, perverted and defiling movies and music, legislating God out of schools, politics, government. It is then you will begin to see the flood, landslides, heat waves, earthquakes and the rivers either drying up or taking its old course!

Eye, ear and skin diseases will resurface and worsen. (Jeremiah 2: 17) Man's ways defile the very economy of a nation. It stops growth and prosperity.

Mismanagement and unfair distribution of the earth's resources – gold, silver and so on – through greed, as well as the mis-treatment of the poor all contribute to climate change significantly and this is what they should be discussing and making active efforts to change.

Believe it or not even our very negative words affect and can destroy the earth. (Hebrews 11; Proverbs 18: 22)

Greed

Trees are being cut down unnecessarily. The reef is being disrupted, unnecessary dredging is taking place, all under the guise of economic development! Many countries are ignoring regulations which are affecting environmental safety. Toxic waste is continually being dumped into the sea! Nuclear and weapons testing and other dangerous tests by world powers are now destroying our marine life.

Our seafood and our sea water are no longer safe. If the minority continues to control the wealth and things continue as they are, then we will further destroy the very thing that God gave man to manage. (Genesis 1: 26; Genesis 2: 15)

The Bible is our God-given operational manual to manage earthly affairs. Everything is in it, including how to avoid certain catastrophe. Even our agriculture has suffered. Let us recognize that everything is connected; and as such, Leviticus 25: 3 – 5 reminds us that a day is given for man to rest, so even the earth must rest. There needs to be a global regulatory body to police scientists and developers as well as undersea activities including certain blasting and digging! So much is being destroyed under the banner of Science and Economic Development – including valuable watershed areas. Some of the fertilizers being used are destroying the earth!

Many nations seek to remove what they view as religion from their grand plans regarding the environment. However, they must recognize that excluding God and His instructions regarding the management of the resources of which HE has given us charge will come back to haunt us in no uncertain terms and we will all have to face it again if it is not resolved.

Climate Change: World Crisis

Climate change is now affecting everyone at this time. It is even affecting national economies and daily life in general.

UN Chief Antonio Guterres called on governments "... to stop building new coal plants by 2020, cut greenhouse emissions by 45% over the next decade and overhauling fossil fuel-driven economies with new technologies like solar and wind. The world, he said, "is facing a grave climate emergency."

The heat waves that have been occurring in different parts of the globe are cause for concern; and this will negatively affect the poor especially regarding health costs and energy consumption. The homeless who have no shelter will also be negatively and directly affected. So, there needs to be emergency funding made available to the poor.

Now is the time funding and subsidies should be made available to the poor and those in rural areas. This will help small business to cope with the high energy costs that will arise.

The priority must now be to plant more trees and relocate those who are closer to highly forested areas in order to prevent tragedy through fires. Nations also need to establish more water wells to deal with this crisis, as the excessive heat will require more water usage. Furthermore, the ground water will disappear and we have the opportunity now to collect it before it does.

What has happened in India - where it's sixth (6th) largest city has run out of water with almost ten (10) million people are without water - should be a lesson to us all.

Tourism Fallout

Nations need to stop the lip service and begin to put serious emergency plans in place, especially for tourism fallout. This is especially true for the Caribbean and Latin American nations.

More people will want to go to cooler destinations. Places like Russia, Alaska, Norway, Holland and their tourism numbers will begin to increase as the world weather crisis will intensify. This is not good for the investors.

The water shortage has the potential to affect hotels, prisons, schools, hospitals, shelters. It can also affect airports and trigger shutdowns.

Urgent plans need to be put in place to prevent the spread of disease particularly where the viruses or bacteria thrive in heat.

Also, additional Fire Trucks, Water Storage Tanks and improved water facilities, as well as portable tanks are needed, as the poor, small children and the elderly are always the most vulnerable.

Farmers

It is reported that thirty-seven percent (37%) of the honeybee colonies were lost over the winter. Honey supply to producers of cereals, some medicines and drinks is significantly affected.

Contingencies and emergency plans need to be put in place for farmers because the heat and the floods as well as hail and the wintry weathers have the potential to seriously and irreversible affect the Agricultural Industry, Livestock and the Fishing Industry.

Water Facilities

More Water Parks need to be set up for children to make use of as they play outside. It will keep them hydrated and less susceptible to the heat waves. Further to this, there is technology that allows water to be pumped every time children use the playground and that is something worth looking into, if we are serious about addressing this crisis.

In addition to all this, we must remember that this kind of crisis has the potential to push up already rising oil prices, food costs and practically every cost that we can incur as human beings. So it is a dire situation that needs to be addressed with great urgency.

Divine Intervention

We cannot address climate change unless we decide to include the One Who made the climate. Luke 21: 25 – 26, 2 Corinthians 7: 13, 2 Kings 8: 35 - 36 and Revelation 16: 21 speak to us about the distress within the earth especially regarding climate change. There are also things that we need to know affects climate change. For example, prayer has a positive effect on the climate; as does atonement. Most countries are trying to legislate the Creator out of their nation.

During such urgent times, the focus ought not to be on dealing with the climatic issues through science only; but we must include a wider cross-section of individuals and deal with the matter holistically.

Real Climate Change

The recently concluded 2021 United Nations Climate Change Conference, more commonly referred to as COP26, has brought some serious issue back into focus.

There cannot be any real discussion about Climate Change if we are going to exclude God - the Author and Creator of the Climate. Most countries are focusing on the wrong thing; hence their nations' resources are being channeled into the wrong areas and are wasted.

Why are we so concerned about carbon emissions while ignoring the other things nations are actively engaged in that are destroying the planets. Instead, nations should be drafting resolutions to prosecute those who are deliberately polluting our oceans and seas the aqua life that call them home. They should extend that punishment to those destroying our reefs and tampering with the environment and atmosphere. That would include those who say they are attempting to block the sun.

God has created the earth perfectly and has given man the stewardship of this planet. So, man is responsible for the management of the earth and the resources within the earth. The seasons are also areas with which man continues to tamper.

Sin

Sin is the number one element that negatively impacts climate change and, if we continue to ignore sin, then everything they are putting on the table to deal with "Climate Change" will come to naught. What man has done and continues to do in the globe, makes significant impact on the climate and ultimately upon Climate Change.

In 2 Chronicles 7: 13 – 14, which says, "When I shut up heaven and there is no rain, or command the locusts to devour the land, or send pestilence among My people, if My people who are called by My name will humble themselves, and pray and seek My face, and turn from their wicked ways, then I will hear from heaven, and will forgive their sin and heal their land", the Lord is reminding us that whenever man misses the target, the action in which must engage is Atonement.   Sin is the biggest threat to Climate Change.

The Way We Treat The Poor

Interference with God's Creation by the Scientists opens the door for serious environmental and spiritual repercussions that will affect creation.   Isaiah 24: 5 – 6 remind us that when we transgress against God's Laws, it changes the ordinance, breaks everlasting covenants, cause tribulation and the violation of God's Word defiles the earth.   Matthew 24: 21 says, "fire will begin to burn, because of the curse. (Revelation 14 – 3; Ezekiel 38: 22). Many will be killed and God will rain fire and brimstone upon all those who have an anti-Christ agenda.

Jeremiah 2:7 shows us that defilement comes in many ways. Sadly, many of the countries that are speaking the most about Climate Change are the ones behind much of what is happening with the climate. How are we going to speak about Climate Change, when the problem lies in some of the policies that are promoted globally. For example, abortion, sexual immorality, witchcraft and population control.

The neglect of the poor also has a negative impact on Climate Change, as many of the poor cannot find basic food items.   This situation is being ignored by many countries.

Negative words spewed into the atmosphere also negatively affects the climate.

Repentance is the biggest solution, but it doesn't make sense to repent if we are not willing to change.

The word for "repentance" in Hebrew is "teshuva" which means "to rearrange your entire way of thinking, your feelings in order to forsake that which is wrong."

When man turns from evil and returns to good, we will see a time of refreshing in the earth, according to Acts 3: 19. We need to be honest regarding Climate Change and repent of the harm that we have caused. We need to get on the new path. If you are driving and you realize that you are on the wrong path, what do we do, do we continue driving or do we change direction? As far as Climate Change is concerned, when we change we will not only save billions of dollars, but we will also save lives. We can then take that money saved and use it to have better infrastructure, (such as River Re-training) for the poor; and this would include education, food, and relocation of the poor from low-lying areas.

Let us be honest with ourselves and with each other and do what needs to be done for real Climate Change to take place.

Chapter 25

PURGING THE BODY OF CHRIST

The Lord has been revealing that He is ready to purge the Body of Christ. Purging is necessary so that we can give Him the offering of pure, holy praise and true worship, in accordance with Malachi 3: 3 which says, "He will sit as a refiner and a purifier of silver;
He will purify the sons of Levi, and purge them as gold and silver, that they may offer to the Lord an offering in righteousness."

God wants true repentance from His people, and if God is going to judge the world, then judgement must begin in the Church first.

The Purpose of Purging

Purging brings fruit, faithfulness, and acceptable worship before God. He wants to purge the sinful ways out of His people – the poor attitudes and pitfalls, the rebellious ways and the disobedience so that He will receive full submission. There are even people within the Body of Christ who think they know more than their leaders. So even when their leaders gives them instructions to pass on to the people, they would change the instructions to the people as they saw fit.

Purging brings growth and when there is no growth God has to prune. (John 15) Purging is like taking a bitter 'washout'. David said in Psalm 51 that God should purge him with hyssop – a bitter bush, for him to be clean. God wants to wash us with His blood for us to be clean. Hyssop was a herb associated with cleansing and purification; symbolically it means cleansing the soul.

The Hebrew word for *wash* is not the one used for a simple cleaning of a dish in water, but rather washing of the clothes by beating. David was asking for a thorough cleansing of the soul. (Numbers 19: 6) Psalm 51: 11 reveals that we must ask God to cleanse us so that He will not cast us out of His Presence – which is the absence of His Spirit.

Psalm 51: 16 tells us that ritual sacrifice or any other religiosity without a change of attitude within the inner man falls short of true repentance. God is ready to deliver us and purge us, but only those with a broken spirit and a broken and contrite heart.

Purging of the Prophet & Prophetic Ministry

One has to be honest with God. (Isaiah 66: 1 – 2). The focus should never be on a physical building, but the spiritual temple. Psalms 34: 18 says: *"The Lord is near to those who have a broken heart and saves such as have a contrite spirit."* We want God to be near to us and we need Him to save us.

In Psalm 51: 6, David said He wanted truth within him – not only in the inward parts but also in the hidden part – the soul. David wanted to be clean and wanted God to purge Him so that He would line up with the Word.

Isaiah 6: 7 says: "And he touched my mouth with it, and said: *"Behold, this has touched your lips; your iniquity is taken away, and your sin purged."*

So it was necessary for Isaiah to be purged so that he could fulfill his purpose, and also that his eyes would open to see the unclean lips and the unclean lifestyle that existed in his environment. He knew that a sinful man in the presence of God would be doom if there was no holiness. So he wants us to know that God's innermost nature is Holiness. Holiness requires separation. For many Christians, there is no distinction between their ways and the world's ways. God wants to break the strongholds. There are many within the prophetic ministry, who are accurate, but are living sinful lives – sexual impurity, gossip, and open sin – church leaders sleeping with or living (unmarried) with church members. This is why moral cleansing must take place in the heart of every sinner, and this can only be done through the shed blood of the Lamb of God. When Christians sin, that hinders other people from coming to God.

Vessels of Honor

2 Timothy 2: 21 – 22 tells us that Christian teachers and leaders are to be righteous in character and conduct, and that only in righteous will they be fit for God's work. To resist temptation is to flee from it, and we must pursue the following:

301

- ✓ **Righteousness**
- ✓ **Faith**
- ✓ **Love**
- ✓ **Peace**

God wants us to flee from sin and pursue holiness.

Throughout our lives as Christians, we either move from or toward something that peaks our interest. You either chase or you are being chased. We must set goals and Godliness must be our goal. So if that is so, then holiness, faith, love, peace and righteousness will be what we pursue. Put those goals on your wall or mirror.

1 Corinthians 5: 6 & 8 speaks about immorality and how it defiles the church. The Corinthians at that time were very tolerant and compromising of the immoral behavior in their midst due to the environment in which they lived. It was the norm to live immorally and they also had a false notion of what God's grace was about – they took God's grace for granted. Sons were sleeping with their fathers' wives and so on. Paul, in the book of Corinthians, was saying that sin – the leaven – had spread, and by all counts, if sin is left unchecked it will spread.

In the Bible, *leaven* is almost always symbolic of sin. Ordinarily, leaven is any substance, (for example, yeast or baking powder) that causes fermentation and expansion of dough or batter. So, like *leaven* that permeates the whole lump of dough, sin will spread in a person, a church, or a nation, eventually overwhelming and bringing its participants into its bondage and eventually to death (Galatians 5:9). Romans 6:23 tell us that "the wages of sin is death," which is God's judgment for sin, and this is the reason that Christ died—to provide a way out of this judgment for sin if man will repent of his sins, accept Christ as his Passover sacrifice, and have his heart changed so that he can conform his life to what God commands.

Recognizing all this, know that there is nothing that the Blood of Jesus can't wash away; it is the "App" for sin.

The Rising Of The Spirit Of Incest

2017 is a very significant year for every believer to rise up and fulfill their God-given purpose. We must walk in obedience according to Deuteronomy 28: 1 – 14 in order to receive the promise. Many persons have great expectations, but those will only come to fruition if we begin to change some things about ourselves now.
  ➢ We have to renew our minds daily
  ➢ Let our light shine
  ➢ Seek God daily
  ➢ Obedience to the instructions of the Lord

Prophetic Revelation

The Lord is showing me that the spirit of Incest will rise – especially that fathers will want to have sex with their daughters and uncles with their nieces. It is happening right across the board with families to destroy the institution of family and many are afraid to talk. We need to rise up against this spirit that is rising up to destroy the family.

We also need to deal with the spirit of incest which is also destroying the church. Pastors and Bishops are 'feasting' on the flock so-to-speak and many of the churches sweep it under the carpet while they allow them to remain on the pulpit. But they must remember I Timothy 3.

God is going to expose more of these issues. If we are the church and we are supposed to bring healing to the world, then it must start within the church. The spirit of Eli has to be broken and HOLINESS must reign if we are going to deal effectively with Perversion and the Spirit of Incest.

- ✓ We also need to cry out against the Media, Hollywood who are promoting perversion and incest. It is extremely rampant, especially among Caucasians.

- ✓ Pray for Maryland. Pray against riots in Indianapolis

- ✓ Pray for the state of Alaska, as government officials are planning to go there regarding oil – potential problems.

- ✓ Pray for the souls of Beyoncé, Kim Kardashian, Lady Gaga, Jamaican singer Sanchez and Boy George.

- ✓ Pray also against a freak accident on Usain Bolt. He needs to seek the Lord and turn his life over to the Lord now.

✓ Single Christians need to read the story of Ruth in the Bible again and line up accordingly.

✓ Pray against meteorites creating havoc and against severe cosmic activities.

✓ Donald Trump needs to be wise regarding Russia. Russia is not his friend. There is a subtle plan to trap him and it can cause impeachment and topple his presidency. He needs to seek God as never before. The enemy will not come in a way to which he is accustomed. They are coming in suits and ties.

Chapter 26

HIGH ALERT IN 2022

Haggai 2: 6 says, *"For thus says the Lord of hosts: 'Once more (it is a little while) I will shake heaven and earth, the sea and dry land;".*

2022 started out on an interesting note with many situations brewing, and towards the end of the 2nd month, the Ukraine/Russia conflict materialize and since became a war. Thus, those who were

The term *"high alert"* simply means *"to be ready for strong possibility of an attack or something dangerous happening."* It is critical for us – God's people and the World – to be on high alert in this time.

Times and Seasons are critical for us to know, and as children of God, we do not operate as the world does. We must depend on the Holy Spirit, who will reveal all things that lie ahead. He will also reveal to us how to prepare and how to make plans.

Weather Threats

The first high alert situation is the global weather patterns. We will see shifts in the weather systems in various parts of the world. As the weather evolves it almost seems as if the climate itself is fighting back, because of the sinfulness of mankind.

The Book of Genesis outlines how sin not only affects those around us, but also the climate. We have seen experiments that have gone wrong because of scientific "intervention" into our God-given environment.

Instability will begin to take place within the cosmos – as in Psalm 46 – tsunamis, earthquake, volcanic eruptions, floods and landslides. (Read also 2 Chronicles 7: 13-14).

Also, we will see an economic reset will take place, and so this will be a year of release. (Hebrews 12: 27).

As the shaking continues, transformation will take place. God is shaking ad removing the man-made systems, because mankind has become evil. We will see the manifestation of the Glory of God in the earth. Scientists will be baffled as many of the shakings and flooding will take place without prior warning. In fact, it is critical for every person to seek the Lord before traveling from place to place, as they may travel and cannot return, and it may result in loss of life, record insurance payouts, infrastructural damage, budget breaking price increases.

War/Terrorism

The next high alert situation is War/Terrorism, and intercessors must be on the wall to pray that our security forces will be on high alert as well.

There cannot be any peace without Jesus Christ. Our security will not be effective unless the Lord build the house. (Psalm 127). Many nations excluded God from their security, and many of them are depending solely on man-made devices – Artificial Intelligence (AI) and robots – which cannot protect us. Our help must come from the Lord in 2022. (Psalm 91, Psalm 121) A leopard never changes its spots, so all nations must be on high alert. It is critical that we seek God to help us identify the true enemy and their plans.

The Health Industry

The state of the Health Industry is the next high alert situation.

It is funny that many media and social network entities are censoring those who speak about anything to do with health, vaccines and viruses, particularly (but not only) when solutions are forthcoming.

Didn't God create man? Are you saying that God does not know what to do or how to fix what has gone wrong? Why aren't they being blocked themselves, because they are the ones giving inaccurate and unreliable information?

Everybody wants to go back to normal, but at the rate they are going, we may not see normal any time soon. There are many lies and deceptions floating around today.

Finance and Food

This next high alert situation is significant. We need to prepare ourselves for the food shortage that will be taking place, and furthermore, the financial and black markets will crash.

Solutions

- ✓ Look for new opportunities

- ✓ Focus on land, real estate

- ✓ Practice Biblical Principles, including Tithing.

- ✓ Stockpile/Store all necessary basic items

- ✓ Dig wells, purchase seed and begin to focus on farm

- ✓ Watch out for animals that may be spreading the virus

- ✓ Be on the alert for other variants of the coronavirus

- ✓ Avoid crowded areas

- ✓ Pray for all bridges, major transportation systems; all places of interest globally and pray for every plan of the enemy to come to naught.

Be alert.

Caribbean In Danger Of Dislocation

Never before have the Caribbean islands been so close to plunging over and into the economic, environmental and social precipice, and currently, are in danger of being dislocated.

For years the Caribbean region, and particularly the CARICOM nations, have been warned to get their proverbial house in order, and to have a plan for the region, in order to remain strong. However, they seem to miss the opportunities to do so, while continuing to make deals and covenants with nations who do not have the region's best interests at heart. They need to understand that most nations see us a banana republic – third world small people who are beggars and a strain on their "first world" economy.   Sadly, there are some within the Caribbean who want to achieve first world status by selling the birthright of the nation.

Further to this, it is utterly embarrassing to see our leaders in the region be reverted to salesmen, to sell products to our people which are only in their preliminary form; putting the lives of those in the region at great risk.

Caribbean leaders have become power-hungry and have allowed their pride, and arrogance to hinder the progress and success of the nation.

With so many brilliant people coming out of the Caribbean region and institutions of higher learning. The COVID-19 pandemic has exposed the failures of our leadership within the region.   Many were begging for vaccines and handouts, when we have the opportunity to develop our own cure.

CARICOM came into being on July 4, 1973 with the signing of the Treaty of Chaguaramas by Prime Ministers Errol Barrow for Barbados, Forbes Burnham for Guyana, Michael Manley for Jamaica and Eric Williams for Trinidad and Tobago.

The Caribbean region has been blessed with good weather, natural resource – herbs, spices, beaches and the best water by far. However, our strongest pillar is the faith of the people in God. Unfortunately, we have allowed nations to capitalize on the laid back approach of our people.

The Greatest Threat

The Caribbean region has some serious threats levied against it, including:

- The new wave of communism rising
- The science-driven approach to governance
- The repackaging of colonialism
- Population Control
- Land Grabbing
- Climate Change – potential tidal waves, tsunamis, cyclones, earthquakes and more;

and these threaten major areas within the region including:

- Religious Rights
- Parental Rights
- Human Rights
- The Nuclear Family
- Migration
- Refugee Protection

and many of these can lead to economic collapse and regional relocation.

Things To Think About

Implementation without Consideration will cause Global Dislocation.

Education without Spiritual Revelation will cause Suffocation

The Lord is reminding us that our Choices always carry good and bad consequences. Our Choices can advance us or cause us to regress. Choices must always be made after seeking God first. (Matthew 6: 33). Let us pray for Jamaica and all the Caribbean Islands, the United States of America, Canada, the United Kingdom, and all the other G7 nations, that they will seek God to deal with the devastation that is coming.

Immediate Action Needed

Repentance stops dislocation and disaster. Nation leaders in the Caribbean need to stop accepting monetary payouts and tell the people of their nations the truth. Furthermore, they need to stop thinking about themselves only and think about the future of their people and the nation.

1. The spirit of the lord says the first thing is true repentance-everyone has to get their houses in order spiritually and naturally.

2. Declare state emergency once this happens

3. Before this happens, stockpile canned foods, water, wipes (of all kinds), toiletries, sanitizers [hand, clothing, and kitchen], sheets, baby foods, baby wipes, towels, bath rags, ply board, baby diapers, toddler pull-ups, socks, undergarments, clothing, detergents, baby bottles, feminine napkins, adult diapers, and bath soaps. Also stockpile rubbing alcohol, first aid kits, toothbrushes, toothpaste, water boots, raincoats, flash lights, lamps, garbage bags including commercial type bags, deodorants, cotton swabs, skin care creams, Q-tips, masks and gloves.

4. After this happens, relocation of those alive to other countries (USA and Canada) where possible.

5. There will need to be relocation of persons living in low lying and other flood-prone areas.

Peoples of the nations, keep stockpiling!

Chapter 27

CRISIS

When there is a crisis - whether in a nation or in the life of an individual, the key actions to take are to enquire and inquire. We must inquire of the Lord what is the cause and enquire concerning what action should be taken and what is the solution.

Every leader in every sector of society must learn from King David in the Bible. He always inquired of the Lord each time he faced enemies, plagues, viruses, famine, adversity or obstacles. David inquired and enquired of the Lord:

- In War
- During Economic Downturn and Famine
- In Recovery Operations
- When He Sinned by taking the Census
- When conspiracy rose against him from his own family

(Read: 1 Samuel 22: 10; 1 Samuel 23: 2; 1 Samuel 30: 18; 2 Samuel 5: 19; 2 Samuel 21: 1; 2 Samuel 24: 1; 1 Chronicles 13: 3)

Take note that when David took the Census, it was a sin simply because His trust was now being place in man rather than maintaining total dependence on and trust in God. As a result of that sin brought plagues and viruses upon and under his administration. However, when he enquired and inquired of the Lord, the Lord gave Him the solution

Do you realize that a greater part of the problem being experienced by the globe in general is a result of not enquiring nor inquiring of the Lord? Man makes many decisions, exclude God and then we all end up in crisis, debt and hopelessness.

God has a plan, but His plan is not always our plan. God will reveal His plans and solutions once we seek and obey Him.
God has been speaking in many ways - even to the world leaders; but they are not listening to Him. Saul lost his crown because He refused to enquire/inquire of the Lord. If they do not listen, many will be brought to a place of humility and humiliation, and they will have no one to blame but themselves.

How many global leaders are willing to enquire and inquire of the Lord:

- ✓ The cause of the current crisis
- ✓ The solution for the crisis
- ✓ What to do to stop the crisis

Maybe they feel more secure enquiring and inquiring of their "expert" advisors and continue to follow the "script" they created.

Unless we enquire and inquire of the Lord, then we may create a problem that we will not be able to handle three months from now.

Important World Solutions

Disaster Solutions

Those with massive investments in the agricultural industry will suffer great losses as a result of the disasters and it will cause a massive shortage in food including, peanuts, potatoes and other vegetables. This will cause a major famine throughout the world. But, the Lord says, "If My people who are called by my name will cry out, then I will show mercy, and My people will be fed during the famine. As they obey Me, worship Me and give their Tithe, they will be protected."

Pray for all places where oil is found and all places where the drilling is taking place, as there will be many disasters. Most of them will crash and workers will be running frantically. It will cause an oil shortage and increase the prices significantly.

We have a crisis and Governments, Businesses and Civil Society now must come together and change their focus. They must begin to focus more on the poor. Many talk about cyber security and this digital era, meanwhile people are not just suffering but are dying as a result of neglect. Cyber, digital and all that will mean nothing when someone is sick and hungry.

Nations need to actively engage in intensive food security programs at both national and individual levels. This extends to protecting marine life, including fish stocks which, given environmental and other threats to the oceans, means the world food supply will diminish even further as world population grows and more natural disasters take place.

Give more support for farming, not only in promoting it as a viable means of income Farming – those in poverty-stricken nations have a low-scale farming. So training is needed for them to improve their farming methods and output. Thus productivity will increase and a market can be established for the produce.

Support the development of micro-industries such as plant nurseries to grow flowers; or water purification plants to produce water for sale, thereby creating employment.

Make warehouse space available for storage of basic items.

Remove tax and customs duties from food items, water, tents and certain basic medical equipment and farmers' tools.

Governments must work with NGOs and Churches to coordinate plans for assistance. There also needs to be more training on issue fueling poverty as well as a harnessing of ideas from the people of the nation.

For years I have been calling for strategic plans for storage of water and food and even Jamaica, should not have designated the Caymanas area for building but for water storage and protection of the natural waters there. Water and food will be critical and we cannot continue to look at climate change from a singular perspective.

Economic Solutions

After taking one tenth of their earnings which is their Tithe, take out another tenth as savings in the event of an economic crash.

- ✓ Revisit insurance policies for their businesses and increase those policies.

- ✓ Stock cases of water, canned items and coal and basins.

- ✓ Give what they can to their community, focus on the poor throughout the island. Set an urgent program which will provide poor families with necessities. Food water shelter clothing and money.

- ✓ Assist with on-the-job training programs and job training programs externally which will open up doors to desired jobs.

- ✓ Assist children in tertiary level education placement (Universities and Colleges).

- ✓ High Schools, Universities and Colleges must have curricula with strong emphasis on Entrepreneurship and Job Creation.

- ✓ Focus more on the P.O.O.R. – Poverty-stricken Outcasts Outsiders and Rejects

- ✓ Investment, Stocks and Bonds, Real Estate Companies, Media Houses, Art Galleries, Credit Unions, Law Firms, Restaurants, Financial Firms – God wants His people to invest in these areas.

Media Houses

Take to the streets more in every parish and change the way they see people.

Design a segment or the poor especially those living on the streets who are neglected by society and genuinely show empathy. Network with other organizations also – NGO's Churches etc. To donate items such as food, clean, quality clothing, socks, shoes, blouses, skirts, dresses, underwear, sandals, building low income houses, visit schools nationwide to speak with children of all ages, asking the children what help they think the church and the government should give, visit various companies of all sizes and do free advertisements for them for at least a week.

Interview workers and clients/customers asking them what they think will help them more effectively as clients/customers and staff.

Chapter 28

GREED AND THE ABSENCE OF LIGHT IN TOURISM

The level of greed that exists within the nation, coupled with the absence of Light within the Tourism sector has caused the nation to be suffering, because they continue to make decisions in the interest of Tourism while the locals are feeling the pangs and taking the blame for the spread of the virus. The decisions being made by those is positions of governance and authority in the different administrations over the years have opened the nation to great suffering for the locals, particularly regarding crime and violence. When other nations closed their borders in an effort to protect its people, we quickly opened ours with very little attention given to safety protocols and occupancy levels. They quickly spread the virus while blaming the locals, then proceeded to lockdown the local businesses and imposed unfair measures on the church, even as the allowed different people to stroll in from different places. While some small sections of the nation benefit from tourism, the majority are not. Tourism has now become the gateway for the anti-Christ system being imposed upon the nation.

In order for Tourism to work there has to be Light. Jesus is the Light and we can't truly prosper or have real success without Him.

Jamaica wants to create a financial hub but it will not successfully come through stocks, bonds and other investment tools. We cannot afford to build tourism on immorality and gambling; that is like building on sand!

We opened our borders and have opened the door to certain nations with little to no requirements because of the hunger for a dollar.

Crime and Violence has spiked.

There is now the introduction of the "Vaccine Passport" which now opens issue of your private health information being made public.

Unreasonable Curfews.   Curfews have now been imposed on locals because of the spike in the virus.

All these things are the results of decisions that were made in the interest of tourism. I was surprised when the news broke about the nation reopening the cruise shipping industry. This will bring more debt, death and hardship on the nation. It is a backward, foolish move that puts all locals at great risk. Even if every passenger took the vaccine, that would not help. In fact, cases would multiply because there is no conclusive, scientific evidence that the vaccine would stop the spread. It does not take much common sense to know that the vaccines being offered are in its preliminary stages, which does not make sense for anyone taking it.

For years the Lord has been warning that Tourism Industry personnel in Jamaica to seek Him before making certain decisions. We were given a great opportunity to reform the way we do tourism by reforming so the locals can benefit. They need to explore new products, but they have failed, and it is costing us more than what we are benefitting as a people. They are relying on immorality to build the nation which is just the same as building on sand.

Solutions

- Make the learning of a second language mandatory in secondary level institutions.

- Use Vale Royal as an historical tourist attraction and pay all future prime ministers a housing allowance.

- The local attractions such as the pantomime and other theatrical and musical programs, must be promoted through the tourism vein so that they can be enjoyed by our visitors!

- Engage in Faith-based Tourism

- Build cottages in our mountains and invest in eco-tourism so that our natural beauty and resources can be preserved while benefiting the tourism industry financially.

- Promote Jamaica as a place for family when people can come and get married and go back home.

- Focus on community tourism as well where the locals can benefit.

- Train our police personnel how to work in the Tourist industry so that security and safety can go to the next level.

Unless we allow the Light to be included in our nation's Tourism sector then we are going to have some painful paths ahead.

Let that sink in.

Fasting: The Unconventional Weapon For Such A Time As This

Fasting is one of the most effective, yet unconventional tools we have to help us achieve success and true prosperity. Solutions, healing and favor for individuals, nations and businesses are some of the benefits of fasting. It also stops judgement on a nation. Once one understands the power and the secret embedded in fasting, then one is already on the right path for success.

Years ago, when I worked at a major organisation, it was faced with serious problems and no one knew what to do. They tried everything and even went as far as inviting expatriates to come and help to solve the problem. A number of jobs were about to be cut as a way of cutting down operational expenses but no solutions were forthcoming. The staff members were instructed to go on a fast. When they did that, immediately transformation took place! The solutions came in abundance and numerous jobs were saved! There was a huge turnaround within the organisation - the fast had brought about tremendous change. The organisation at that time became a model for other companies! Even the trade unions were surprised!

Fasts And Divine Intervention

Can you imagine if the leader of this nation decided to stand up one day and call the other political parties, the public and private-sector leaders together and say, "Let us put our political issues aside and cry out to the Lord for solutions and for divine intervention in this nation?" There would be changes in the economy, the killing of children would cease, the corruption would decrease significantly and there would be solutions and favor upon the nation!

There are different kinds of fasts and a fast can range from one to 40 days.

With all these fasts, there are different levels which include partial, absolute, juice and vegetables fasts. Before you fast, check with your physician and once you have been deemed healthy enough to fast, wash your face, anoint your head and go on the fast.

Fasting has been tested and proven! Many persons - whether religious or not - know that fasting is a tested and proven tool, and that it never fails to accomplish the goal!

Some examples of fasts are:

1-Day Fast
to hear from God and for spiritual examination is found in Genesis 23: 27; Judges 20:18.

1-Day Ezra Fast
for guidance and protection for our children, security for our possession and our businesses is found in Ezra 8:21-23. (This fast will bring God's protection and cut down on crime.)

1-Day Daniel Night Fast
for national leaders dealing with a life-threatening situation in their administration is found in Daniel 6:18.

1-Day Joel 2 Fast
for the turnaround in a nation's economy, to avert judgement, break famine, cut crime and bring new business ideas and improvement to the agricultural sector is found in Joel 2.

1-Day Samuel Fast
for religious leaders to bring victory over the enemy and purge the nation of images and idols is found in I Samuel 7:1-12.

1-Day Isaiah 58 Fast
to break yokes, peace and inner-city renewal and restore the value of real estate is found in Isaiah 58.

1-Day Jonah Fast
to avert disasters (earthquakes, tsunamis and tidal waves) is found in Jonah 3:5-9

3-Day Fast
which brings favor, healing, breakthrough, opens doors and gives God's favor in legal issues is found in I Samuel 30:11-2 and Esther 4.

7-Day Consecration Fast
which brings us into the presence of the Lord and gives us God's favor is found in Ezekiel 43:35-37.

10-day Daniel fast
which brings healing, divine revelation, godly wisdom and deals with witchcraft is found in Daniel 1.

21-day Daniel fast
which brings fresh revelation and solutions, breaks down strongholds over individuals and nations, and releases God's angels over the nation is found in Daniel 10.

40-day fast
is for dominion and power from the Lord is found in Deuteronomy 9:18-21 and Exodus 24:18.

Recognize that if we don't fast, Sunday Worship may become a thing of the past. Rise up and wise up!

Chapter 29

THE GREATEST THREAT TO CHRISTIANITY

Mark 4: 19 says, *"and the cares of this world, the deceitfulness of riches, and the desires for other things entering in choke the word, and it becomes unfruitful."*

The greatest threat against Christianity is *"the cares of the world"*. What would happen of Christians were focusing on and seeking God more than they were the cares of the world. (Matthew 6: 33). Then there would be less struggles and we would be manifesting in dominion! Christians no longer know what belongs to them because they have become lukewarm. The pandemic has revealed the condition of Christianity.

Lukewarm And Lacking Focus

If God cannot get one's focus, how can He get one's attention. We miss God's true blessing daily because of our focus on the cares of the world. As a result, we are eating the crumbs so-to-speak while the world enjoys the blessings that belong to us.

Lack of focus and attention bring lack of growth. The enemy is taking what truly belongs to us and is repackaging it to us to sell it back to us and then behave as if they are doing us a favor.
Most Christians are not fulfilling their purpose because of their focus on the cares of life. They are not in God's will;

hence they are not hearing what God is saying to them nor do they know what God has in store for them. They are operating as the helper when they are supposed to be the master – and that includes the workplace. You will never do great exploits for God if your focus is on the cares of life.

Jesus, in the midst of pain, persecution, lies, rejection, and suffering, never put the Kingdom second. As Christians we pray more on a daily basis than we do for man to come to Christ, and that is why we are experiencing so much evil, problems and greed. Men are becoming more evil as a result of their focus on the cares of life. They are not function the way they ought to do. Christians are spending more hours in the world, and very few minutes in His Presence.

In light of the technological advancements such as the virtual platform, many still come on turning off the camera to hide their face and still attired in their nightgowns or pajamas or less, behaving as if they are doing God a favor.

The Consequences of Being Lukewarm

Revelation 3: 15 – 16 reminds us, "I know your works, that you are neither cold nor hot. I could wish you were cold or hot. So then, because you are lukewarm, and neither cold nor hot, I will vomit you out of My mouth."

One of the consequences of being lukewarm is that you fall into becoming the like the Laodicean Church. Cool

Springs are refreshing; Hot springs are medicinal, but lukewarm springs are nauseating. As a result, being lukewarm simply means you are undesirable, useless and you are creating no fruit nor impact. (Matthew 7: 16 -17). They say they are Christians, but they bear no resemblance to Christ. They serve no purpose in the kingdom, they live like the world, they compromise, they have no faith. They have what we could call "spiritual cataracts". They are unfaithful and have no zeal for the things of God.

Being lukewarm is a spiritual disease from which one needs deliverance. In a lukewarm church one becomes complacent. They have no zeal for prayer nor evangelism. God is knocking at the door, and most are neither hearing nor obeying, nor are they allowing the Lord to come in and dine with them.

Is There Oil In Your Lamp

The Laodicea was noted for being a banking center for the production of a glossy black wool used in clothing and carpets, and for producing salves for caring of eye disorders; and that is why the church is desperately needed. The grace that regenerates the garment of Christ's righteousness, illuminates the spirit and sets us on fire for the Lord to do His work and will is desperately needed once more. Each of us has a lamp in us which represents Christ on the inside of us. We need oil each day to keep our lamps alight. Most lamps are almost out and Matthew 25 reminds us that we need oil in our lamps daily. We are spirit-man in a body of flesh, so our souls have to be continually set ablaze. Many are going to Church just for the sake of going and for occupying different positions, but they have already divorced Christ and they have no intimacy with Him.

If a Christian's passion is not to do the will of God, then something is wrong with that Christian. As a result of being lukewarm, many are missing their inheritance. Are you to busy for God's Presence?

Christians! Write, And Run With The Vision

The pandemic and all that has come with it should be an eye-opener for every Christian on this planet. It should now be clear that your politicians are not your friends, your bank is not your friend, your job is not your friend, nor is it your source. One of the greatest gifts God has given to mankind is not sight, but vision; and as I have often said, vision is a not a function of the eye, but of the heart. Vision allows us to see a future. The lack of vision has allowed global leaders to become enslaved by "Big Tech" and "Big Pharma"!
If Christians are going to survive in this time, and employ others of like mind, we must write the vision and run with what God has given us. Each of us is given a vision to birth and it is key to seek God in prayer and fasting to birth that vision He has given you.

Vision is birthed out of the demand within our nation or community. Remember, problems are gates to change and if you begin to write down the problem within your nation or community that is a start which will lead you to great ideas and solutions.

The Power of Vision

Vision can remove rules, regulations, and manipulation. There are many businesspeople who believe that no one can do without their business – they are monopolies, so they treat people any way they feel like treating them. So, God is looking for visionaries to rise up and begin to make a change.

With the current situation in politics globally, God is looking for visionaries to come forth and to execute the ideas He gives them to save and transform lives – helping the poor, the fatherless, and the widow.

Vision opens doors for new players. It increases jobs, allows for new products and services to come to the fore. It raises new millionaires who understand the value of ALL resources afford them especially human resources and know that they should not use the people as guinea pigs.

Vision creates hope and brings change. It averts danger ahead. For example, if God did not give Joseph a vision to implement for the famine that was coming, then the nation would have died of hunger.

Vision will not be plain or clear to the people without God's guidance, prayer, fasting, repentance and sacrifice.

Many try to achieve success through logical thinking and academic abilities while devoid of faith in God. We are now seeing the results, effects and repercussions of this kind of thinking. Most countries, in order to maintain economic growth, they are now forced to accept the resources and funding of the unclean things to run the nation, which will bring grave consequences going forward.

If vision is about building for the future, and a person can't see the future, how can they build for it? Many are building blindly, and that is the reason that for a lack of vision the people perish. No nation can function without the prophetic revelation.

Every visionary must be in the watchtower to get instruction; and for every vision there is always Provision. Poverty within a nation, is as a result of a lack of vision, and vision is the source if true leadership.
Remember that every vision is birthed through faith and prayer. God is now downloading many things within His people as Babylon is fallen. We need Christian business owners who will deal with a healthy lifestyle and way of living. We need kingdom banking for the kingdom businesses. We need Kingdom Marine Biologists, Kingdom Supermarkets, Kingdom Schools at all levels, we need Kingdom Restaurants, Kingdom Investors, Kingdom Realtors, Kingdom Mortgage Brokers.

Christians need to move fast as the anti-Christ systems are churning out new laws and rules to hinder the advancement of Christians.

Times and Seasons are critical to our success. Who knows what they will be coming with next.

Chapter 30

EXODUS: MOVEMENT OF GOD'S PEOPLE

I have said many times in many of my writings, and it is also revealed in the Bible – the main fact that God has not already shut down some organizations, is that God's people are still there. The COVID-19 Pandemic has revealed the hearts of leaders at every level.

Many staff members far and wide have been given ultimatum to take the vaccine or else be out of a job. Some are also given documents to sign which say that the vaccine is safe and that it is the only alternative against the virus and its variants. So, the questions that I would like answered are Where do we place God amid the pestilence coming against His creation? What about other alternative ways, and alternative medications that can be used to treat the virus – ways and medicines that governments are refusing to try? What about the ibuprofen, ibumetin, supplements and vitamins to build up the immune system? With so many Christians being forced out of the marketplace – including teachers and security personnel, are we ready for the collapse of the workforce?

It is documented in the Bible that when the Children of Israel made an Exodus from the Egyptian systems and economy, there was "lights-out".

It is very foolish to remove light and salt from the workforce. The main fact that God has blessed your business/organization is as a result of the grace and blessing upon His people. If the people go, the grace goes and so does the blessing.

While many will fight and talk about human rights, sexual rights, abortion rights, how is it we don't have people fighting to defend what is going into our bodies? If there is not a change in policy on this issue, the entire workforce will go under, which has the potential to sink economies and fuel famine and starvation.

We should never forget the story of Laban in the Bible, and that it was the blessing on Jacob's life that brought increase in Laban's business. If God can cause a famine to promote one man – Joseph, why do you think He won't do it for His people? God brought barrenness on kings just because they offended His servants.

When man devises laws to oppress God's people by way of forced vaccines for example, they must also prepare for the consequences. If a country can be locked down for many days without regard for sustaining the basic needs of the people, just so they can be "encouraged" to be vaccinated at the open vaccination sites, then why can't we lock down businesses for 7 days to make atonement to God to stop the virus? The Book of Joel says it as well as 2 Chronicles 7: 14.

Be Careful With Christians

It is critical to understand that Christians bring positive virtue, morals, loyalty and solutions within the workplace. So when they go, all the values, good solutions and Divine protection leave with them. Are the forced vaccines a deliberate act to market or sell other products between now and the next 2 years based on the negative occurrence that will result from the fallout since there is no scientific data regarding the potential negative impact of these new drugs?

If we are serious about bringing cures in the pandemic, why are we afraid to have multiple trials of the drugs? Why not carry out post mortems to see the true root cause so scientists can better treat the issue? Why not give doctors the opportunity to use their expertise to treat each patient individually since each person is different? Why are doctors operating on protocols, especially where some of these protocols are unrelated to the scientific? Why are we not advertising anything about those who have recovered nor the recovery rate? Why is the focus only on those who have been affected and are still ill or are dead? Is it a marketing strategy?

Time will tell.

On This Rock I Shall Build My Church

Matthew 16: 18 reminds us, "And I also say to you that you are Peter, and on this rock I will build My church, and the gates of Hades shall not prevail against it."

There is a great move by the secular sector of our society and the secular media to bring news that the Church is declining, and many people are turning away. So, we must ask ourselves, "From which source are they getting the information?"

The Falling Away

While the Bible may speak of the great falling away from the truth in the end times, God is separating the wheat from the tares. 2 Thessalonians 2: 3 refers to the falling away as there will be a massive rebellion against God and His authority by unbelieving believers. These "believers" will hide in the Church but will serve the Anti-Christ in the end times. 2 Thessalonians 2 tells us that Satan will deceive many with his power, signs and lying wonders and with all unrighteous deception. Many refuse to accept the love and truth of God; and because they do so, God Himself will send strong delusions that they will believe the lie. So, anyone who fails to believe the truth – including the four (4) gospels, will instead believe a lie. They will believe false prophets, false christs, false scientists, lying politicians rather than the truth of God.

The Holy Spirit Restraining Power

Only the Holy Spirit's restraining power will keep us from being deceived in the end time by the demonic agenda. We must also take comfort that many who followed Christ, were not for Christ. People followed for various reasons and the same is true today. God, however, has many ways to reveal the hearts of the people and to show which of those following are loyal.

The COVID-19 Pandemic was the perfect platform to test who was loyal to God. Many hearts were revealed. Both Atheists and Secularists need to understand that God's Church never comes second in anything. God's Church Cannot Die!

The Church Is An Organism Not Just An Organization

There is a difference between an organism and an organization. An organization as we understand it, has buildings, chairs and other infrastructure - all of which are lifeless. However, an organism has life - it is a living thing, birthed out of life which also produces life and it is life that powers the organism - the Holy Spirit of God - Who is Life. The Church is a mediator between heaven and earth and the Church belongs to Jesus Christ. So, when viruses and plagues come, don't try to and think you are shutting the Church down, while you leave open organizations which are lifeless - they don't support life nor are they supported by Life.

So, in the midst of a pandemic, famine, pestilence, earthquake and even the rising of the sea, and the closing down of the secular organizations, the Church is still standing! Secular organizations – banks and insurance companies – they are simply that – organizations. They are lifeless. However, the Church is an organism, and as such it is, and perpetuates life. Thus, in due season, many form the lifeless will be coming to seek a job from life and will be coming to life.

The Presence, Power and Glory of God that will manifest in the end time according to Joel 2, will be poured out in the end times regardless of what laws have been put in place to stop God's Church will be useless. The very lawmakers will bow! We are about to see masses coming to the Lord, and the very ones Satan will be using to attack the Church are the ones who will turn and attack the kingdom of darkness.

Do You Know The Remnant?

The media needs to learn about the 11th hour Christians in Matthew 20. They also need to do their research on who the remnant is, and this is why it is key to know which side they are on; they also need to know that Jesus is the Way, the Door, the Truth, the Deliverer, He is Savior, He declared the end from the beginning – He is Alpha and Omega, the First and Last, the Beginning and the End. He rules in the affairs of men. (Jeremiah 23: 3, Jeremiah 31: Romans 9: 27)

The coming Remnant Church with Jesus at Center and as the Center of the Church. They will live holy. They will be watching and waiting for Jesus to return. (Luke 12: 37 – 39). They will be warning the world of sin (1 Corinthians 6: 9 – 10). They will be bold – one heart, one mind. They will be fully loaded with the Holy Spirit. Metaverse and AI will be nothing by comparison. They will be everywhere. So, how can the secular win?

Season Of Pentecost And Prophecies

We are in the season of Pentecost, and Pentecost is one of the greatest seasons for mankind. It is the seasons within which the Church was birthed; and it is about ordinary people being empowered to do extraordinary things. It is a time during which God pours out upon his people.

As we read the book of Acts, we see the manifestation of the power of the Holy Spirit. After Passover, God instructed Israel to number 7 Sabbaths plus 1 day, which worked out to be 49 days plus 1 day which in total is 50 days. The number 50 signifies jubilee, liberty/freedom, and is the number for the Holy Spirit. (Leviticus 25: 10). Now it is important for us to realize that we can do nothing without the Holy Spirit. He is God. If Jesus did not carry out His ministry without the Holy Spirit, what say we as a Church. We need the Holy Spirit of God!

Acts 1: 8 says, *"But you shall receive power when the Holy Spirit has come upon you; and you shall be witnesses to Me in Jerusalem, and in all Judea and Samaria, and to the end of the earth."*

If the Church is going to walk in the Spirit of Excellence, and display God's Divine power, it is critical for us to get back to the Holy Spirit. Many have locked Him out of the Church, while focusing on the world and what it has to offer. A world without the Holy Spirit is just simply chaos and darkness. We have seen both secular and religious leaders fail badly because they have exchanged the

Holy Spirit for other spirits; hence the current global problems we now face.

The Holy Spirit is now pouring out His power and His Spirit upon all those who welcome Him.

There are many benefits we receive at Pentecost – Power, Promotion, Purpose and Provision. It is an Upper Room moment of Prayer

Prophecies

- ✓ For the next 6 months, we need to watch global economies. There will indeed be great shaking of the governments and the Church. Meanwhile, the levels of sin and evil will continue to rise, BUT, the Power of the Holy Spirit will increase and intensify. We will also see natural and spiritual earthquakes taking place.

- ✓ God is calling His people to rise up and tear down the strongholds and evils over and within nations. He is also calling the mothers of Zion to be revived, arise, be refreshed, be empowered and get back on the wall.

- ✓ Global expansion of the Kingdom will be taking place. A time of refreshing, rebirthing and renewal. New wine will be poured from the heavens upon the nations and even more so upon His people.

✓ The Lord says we are to pray and watch France and India. He further said that many of the politicians will be removed from the scene that a number of them will be arrested at the airport. There are going to be major explosions taking place in Space. The Lord also says that there will be a massacre taking place in Jamaica. There will be major investigations among billionaires, and many offices will be raided. Many government offices locally and globally will be raided by Law Enforcement.

✓ There will be major division among politicians and government officials which will lead to great exposure. Some politicians' eyes will be opened but it will be too late – particularly concerning contracts they have signed. There will be a changing of the guard soon – from the top to the bottom. However, it is critical for the globe to pray that there won't be missile attacks on the West. A dying bear is dangerous because they will lash out and they have nothing to lose. The West needs to be warned and be on high alert against attacks.

✓ Many are complaining about the shooting currently taking place in the USA, but the root is being ignored. The root cause is sin. The focus should not only be on the one who pulls the trigger, but on who is behind the trigger-puller.

✓ While they lament about school shootings and gun control, there is major neglect regarding the killing of the unborn child, and while I condone neither, we must give attention to both equally.

✓ The Lord is asking the question – "Who will stand up for the voiceless?"

✓ More schools and campuses will close because of shootings.

✓ We are about to witness the 4 horsemen according to the book of Revelation. Now we will see the pale horse and black horse in effect. The Pale Horse signifies death, disease, water problems, and hunger. The Black Horse signifies food shortages, war, high food prices, scarcity and economic disruption.

✓ There will be a major split within the current political party in government – the like of which has never been seen before. The civilians will begin to express their frustrations and declare that they have had enough.
✓ Hospitals in Jamaica need urgent attention as more supplies will be needed to deal with what lies ahead. They also need more health centers and hospitals within the country. No one should be turned back. Pray for the hospitals.

✓ The Lord says there is a massive wind blowing away the things that are evil.

✓ Many commercial airlines will be grounded and numerous flight cancellations will occur because of what is going on in the atmosphere. The Lord says He is allowing this to protect His people.

✓ The bear has plans to send missiles to the USA.

✓ There are different terrorist attacks that are staged by popular people.

✓ The Lord says there needs to be health discounts for the people.

✓ The Lord also revealed many caskets side by side.

✓ In Jamaica, many buildings will be shaken down including old church buildings.

BIBLIOGRAPHY

Hagee, John C. General Editor, *Prophecy Study Bible*, (New King James Version) © 1997 Thomas Nelson, Inc

Hayford, Jack W. Executive Editor, *New Spirit-Filled Life®️ Bible*, (New King James Version) © 2002 Thomas Nelson, Inc.

Lyston, Steve, *Man, Money, Ministry*, © 2009 Xlibris

Pfeiffer, Charles F., Vos, Howard F., Rea, John. Editors, *Wycliffe Bible Dictionary*, (Seventh Printing) © 2005 Hendrickson Publishers, Inc

Price, Paula A. (PhD). *The Prophet's Dictionary: The Ultimate Guide To Supernatural Wisdom*, © 1999, 2002, 2006 Whittaker House

Strong, James. *The New Strong's Expanded Exhaustive Concordance of the Bible*, (Red Letter Edition) © 1990 Thomas Nelson Publishers

Van Impe, Jack. *Jack Van Impe Prophecy Bible, Special Limited KJV Collector Edition*, (Red Letter Edition) © 1999 Jack Van Impe Ministries

Concise Oxford English Dictionary Eleventh Edition. © 1964, 1976, 1982, 1990, 1995, 1999, 2001, 2004 Oxford University Press. All Rights Reserved.

https://www.attractionfrequency.com/number-8-meaning-in-the-bible/

https://www.science.org/content/article/lab-grown-embryos-mix-human-and-monkey-cells-first-time

https://www.texastribune.org/2019/10/11/beto-orourke-religious-institutions-gay-marriage/

https://news.un.org/en/story/2020/01/1056372